The Jewish Kitchen

RECIPES AND STORIES FROM AROUND THE WORLD

The Jewish Kitchen

RECIPES AND STORIES FROM AROUND THE WORLD

CLARISSA HYMAN

SPECIAL PHOTOGRAPHY BY PETER CASSIDY

Interlink Books

LEFT TO RIGHT: KOSHER DELI,
SAO PAULO, BRAZIL; MAKING
MINA DE MAZA; SESAME
BREAD RINGS; RUGALACH;
APPLES AND WINE

Dedication
To the memory of my beloved parents

First American edition published in 2004 by
INTERLINK BOOKS
An imprint of Interlink Publishing Group, Inc.
46 Crosby Street, Northampton, MA 01060
www.interlinkbooks.com

Publishing Director: Lorraine Dickey
Senior Editor: Katey Day
Assistant Editor: Sybella Marlow
Art Director: Chi Lam
Designer: Megan Smith
Picture Research: Sarah Hopper
Special Photography: Peter Cassidy
Food Stylist: Jacqueline Malouf
Prop Stylist: Róisín Nield
Production Manager: Angela Couchman
Production Assistant: Natalie Moore

Library of Congress
Cataloging-in-Publication Data available

ISBN 1-56656-550-2 (pb)

Printed and bound in China

MAY 0 6 2009

All recipes have been tested with large eggs.
All recipes use unsalted butter.
All recipes have been tested in a standard
(i.e., non-convection) oven.

Matzo meal is available in three grades: medium,
fine and cake meal. Fine and cake meal can be
made by processing medium matzo meal, for 5
and 10 seconds respectively, to the required
consistency.

Schmaltz, rendered chicken fat, is made by
cutting up the fat and fatty skin of a chicken into
small pieces (either obtain the fat from a butcher
or save up the fat in the freezer from several
chickens until you have at least eight ounces).
Heat the chicken fat, either in a very low oven or
in a frying pan over the lowest possible heat until
it melts. Add a sliced onion for flavor, and cook
until the onion and small pieces of skin are crisp
and brown (but not black!). Remove the latter
with a slotted spoon (these are called *gribene* and
can be added to chopped liver). Strain the fat
through a sieve and let stand until cool, but still
liquid. Pour into a jar and refrigerate or freeze.

Contents

Introduction

As this is a Jewish cookbook, I'll start with a Jewish joke. The Brisket Joke. Like many of the recipes in this book, it is tried and tested, but still bears regular repetition. So, don't stop me if you've heard it.

A young Jewish mother is preparing a piece of brisket one day for dinner. Her daughter watches with interest as she slices off the ends of the brisket before placing it in the roasting pan, and asks why she did this. The mother pauses and says, "You know, I'm not sure. This is the way I always saw my mother make a brisket. Let's call grandma and ask her."

She phones her mother and asks why they always slice off the ends before roasting the brisket. The grandmother thinks for a moment and then says, "You know, I'm not sure why, this is the way I always saw *my* mother do it." Now they're all very curious, so they pay a visit to great-grandmother in the nursing home.

"You know when we make a brisket," they chorus, "we always slice off the ends before roasting. Why is that?"

"I don't know why *you* do it," replied the old woman, "but my reason was that I never had a pan that was large enough!"

Well, it's only old if you've heard it before, but this cautionary tale tells us something about food and tradition. It makes the point, for example, that cooking is not a rigid practice, that recipes must evolve according to the times and places in which we live, our changing circumstances and our personal tastes and skills. One friend, who offered me a recipe, said she originally gave it to a cousin, then it worked its way around the family until it was finally passed right back to her (slightly changed, of course. No Jewish cook can resist a little, how shall I put it, improvement?).

It also warns us against regarding the past with unquestioning reverence. Of course, we all know our grandmothers were expert shoppers who had tremendous strength of character, the physical stamina and infinite patience to hand-chop, hand-beat, hand-whip, hand-grate everything from gefilte fish to grains of couscous. But although there was reminiscence in every bite they took, a belief that everything (sigh) was better in the "old country," most of them were only too glad to embrace labor-saving technology, much as we, in our turn, do today.

On the other hand, the story emphasizes that certain dishes can act as bonds that tie the family together and link the generations in deep, emotional ways. Tradition may be a *Fiddler on the Roof* cliché, but tradition still tugs at the heart strings and shapes the passage of the years. In our minds, a haze of nostalgia hovers over the Jewish kitchen like the steam from a pot of simmering soup.

Nostalgia, of course, isn't what it used to be, but it can still play culinary tricks. Another joke tells of the man who kept complaining that his wife's chicken never tasted as good as that made by his mother. One day, in sheer annoyance, she served it up burned and blackened. "At last," he exclaimed with delight, "You've made it exactly right!"

So, Jewish cooking is more, far more, than just food on a plate. It is a map of the past, as well as a continuing story of religion, history, culture and family life. It is also a portable concept, a statement

of identity that journeys in mental baggage across continents, war-zones and social upheaval, through good times and bad, emigration and re-settlement, into exile and back – a place of refuge in times of trouble. Sometimes that baggage takes physical form – the heavy iron casserole dish or brass mortar and pestle transported to a new life in a new land; mostly it is an expression of family values, an assertion of stability in a world of chaos.

Jewish cooking has often been a constant as Jewish cooks have repeatedly crisscrossed the globe, fleeing from persecution and prejudice, in search of physical safety, economic security and religious freedom. In the worldwide Jewish Diaspora, traditional foods are a taste of home – sometimes an ancient biblical home, sometimes a place in Eastern Europe, the Levant or Spain that was home for centuries. And in the homeland of Israel, these foods are still celebrated alongside and incorporated into an emerging, vibrant new national cuisine.

Like the braided candle that is lit to say farewell to the Sabbath and so separate the sacred from the everyday, Jewish cooking reflects the diverse strands of Jewish history and dispersal: Ashkenazi (Jews of mostly central and eastern European descent), Sephardi (of Spanish and Portuguese origin), and Mizrahi (of North African and Middle East origin), plus others such as the Jews of Italy, Yemen, Ethiopia, India and Central Asia. Jewish food, on one level, is the food eaten by Jewish people, and for centuries that has reflected the food of the countries where they have stopped or settled.

This book, indeed, reflects the fact that the Jewish Diaspora spans the globe, each community taking on the culinary color and shading of its hosts, borrowing ingredients and adapting techniques to suit the constraints of the Jewish kitchen. Gefilte fish is a classic example – the nature of the fish changing as patterns of Jewish migration forced the housewife to make use of whatever fish was locally available. German zimtsterne biscuits, for example, are eaten by non-Jews at Christmas, by Jews at Rosh Hashanah; fried sardines stuffed with herbs are popular with Moroccans of every denomination. From the borscht and blintzes of Eastern Europe to the spicy fish and couscous of North Africa, from Latin American picadillo, rich with vibrant flavoring, to the unique rice dishes of Central Asia, the Jewish kitchen is dazzlingly diverse, an edible coat of many colors.

Not that the trade was always one-way: the Jewish presence has left its mark on the way in which Italians cook artichokes *alla giudea*, for example; in the UK the origin of fried fish and chips in oil is attributed to Jewish influence and ingenuity. The differences, however, between the Jewish and non-Jewish worlds have always been more significant than the similarities, perhaps because every act in the Jewish kitchen, as in Jewish life as a whole, is imbued with a greater meaning.

Kashrut, the dietary laws that define what Jews can and cannot eat, is the common thread that has kept the kosher kitchen separate from its fellows. Even when Jewish cooks in various parts of the world produce dishes unrecognizable to each

other, their cuisine is still based on common function and shared religious tradition, rather than on a single geographical area. With very few exceptions, what is kosher in one part of the world is kosher everywhere else, and the food taboos are deep and powerful, almost visceral. Sometimes, as at the time of the Inquisition, Spanish and Portuguese "Marranos" (Jews forced to convert or face death) were "exposed" for their lack of faith because they would not cook with pork fat or made their adafina casserole on Friday to avoid cooking on the Sabbath; half-way across the world, the Jews of Yemen adhered to all the precepts of kosher cooking, despite their centuries of isolation.

Every Jewish family today has its own level of observance, but even when food is the final remnant of faith, there are still boundaries, such as spreading a chopped liver sandwich with butter, beyond which Jewish cooking loses its essence and very soul (not to mention the fact it simply could never taste right). Jewish children quickly learn what is permitted and what is not, a knowledge that is acquired alongside what the social historian Ruth Gay has called "a palette of tastes, with its distinctive smells and textures." As she says, however much the assimilated Jew may depart from the chosen path, hidden in each head is an original tuning fork that demands the comfort of chicken soup (or eggplant borrekitas or beef with okra…) on a dark winter day.

More fundamentally, Kashrut, as well as separating Jew from non-Jew, is a constant reminder of how the divine interacts with daily existence. As Maimonides argued, the dietary laws "train us in the mastery of our appetites. They accustom us to restrain both the growth of desire and the disposition to consider the pleasures of eating as the end of man's existence." Some rabbis in the Talmud went even further: to eat non-kosher food, they said, would "clog up the pores of your soul."

Food, indeed the very act of eating, is never to be taken for granted. The Jewish home is seen as a reminder of the destroyed Temple, the kitchen its sanctuary and the table its altar, above all on the Sabbath. As such, food is both physical and spiritual nourishment, to be consumed with respect and gratitude. As well as blessings for different foods, there are blessings both before and after the meal, for as the Book of Deuteronomy says: "And you shall eat and be full and you shall bless…." Every meal is, in a sense, a religious ceremony that has helped preserve both faith and family.

If Kashrut is the frame that holds Jewish food together, then the Sabbath and festivals are the nails that keep it in place. Throughout the world, Jewish families have always held to, and been united by, the special foods that mark the passage of the weeks and year: the Sabbath challah bread, the dairy dishes for Shavuot or fried ones at Hanukkah. The obligations of these holy days have also helped define the nature of the Jewish kitchen: slow-cooked casseroles or cold fish dishes, for example, that avoid the need to cook (i.e., work) on the Sabbath; the ingenious dishes, such as mina de maza, or Swiss carrot cake that use matzo and matzo meal instead of bread and flour during Passover.

LEFT TO RIGHT: MATZO CLASS, MANCHESTER, ENGLAND; KOSHER PARIS; MAKING MINA DE MAZA

Celebration or commemoration, food is always part of the ritual. There may be a multitude of fascinating variations on the theme, but the similarities are the greater force for communal solidarity and religious cohesion. This is, in part, because of Kashrut and the religious calendar, but also because Jewish food is often inspired by biblical symbolism, Talmudic word-play and mysterious layers of meaning, shot through with spiritual yearning.

Jews have always talked a lot about food, partly because dietary prohibitions intensify the pleasure of the permitted (the meal after the Yom Kippur fast, for example), and partly because historically it was often so lacking in their lives. Jewish mothers were always adept at making a little go a long way, scrimping and saving to be able to celebrate the holidays with the choicest foods; many individual dishes retain the simplicity of poverty, hardship and affliction. Indeed, Jewish writers would often fantasize about tasty dishes because they were "so poor, there was no money for water over the kasha." It is perhaps one reason why Jewish cooking so often mixes the bitter or sour with the sweet. The Yiddish saying *bitterer gelechter* (bitter laughter), describes the humor to be found in the worst of situations… but the bitterness is always there. In food, as in life.

Today, however, the sophisticated kosher consumer is able to take advantage of sophisticated kosher products that blur the boundaries and make the kosher kitchen as up to date and as inclusive as any other, but this book is not about nouveau Jewish nor kosher-lite cooking, Jewish sushi, mock shrimp cocktail or bacon substitutes. Neither is it a first-find-the-kitchen manual. Nor is it 1,001 things to do with a piece of chicken. Nor, with some exceptions, especially the ones given to me by several talented young Israeli chefs, is it about giving an innovative twist to classic recipes. No, there are already many wonderful Jewish cookbooks that do these jobs far better than I ever could.

In a popular satirical newspaper column in Salonika in the 1930s, that depicted the comic fictional trials and tribulations of an everyday Sephardi family, the feisty, sharp-tongued Benuta demonstrated her contemptuous disdain for new-fangled "inedible" Western dishes such as sardines with butter, and cauliflower with mayonnaise, adding, for good measure: *Las balabayas de agora son kuzineras kon livro* (the housewives of today are book-cooks). *Adiosanto*!

Guilty, Benuta, but in defense, as I cannot be by your side in the kitchen, as oral memories fail and domestic life deconstructs, books like this must continue to be written. So, this *Jewish Kitchen* is largely about traditional family dishes, passed from one cook to another or handed down through the generations. Many of these recipes came with instructions to include "ein bisl dis, ein bisl dat" (a little this, a little that)… and I have tried to keep them in character without turning back the clock. Some updating has been necessary, but I hope they remain true to the spirit of the originals.

In my research for this book I opened an old 1930s cookbook that had belonged to my mother and a crumpled piece of paper

LEFT: A HASSIDIC CELEBRATORY MEAL; RIGHT: DINNER AT THE CORREA FAMILY'S HOUSE IN THE SCHAARLOO QUARTER OF CURAÇAO, 1930

fell from the torn, yellowing pages. A fragment from a forgotten life, it was a long-forgotten recipe for home-pickled herring, beautifully transcribed in copperplate handwriting, but with no other clue to its origin or author. An epitaph for an unknown housewife. Such recipes are endangered in every culture and tradition; it is a testament to the strength of Jewish family life that so many have endured for so long.

It is also why I felt it important to record the context of the recipes of *The Jewish Kitchen*. This is nothing new, of course. Joan Nathan and Gil Marks in the US and Claudia Roden and Evelyn Rose in the UK, in particular, have all made hugely distinguished contributions to the history of Jewish food. This book is a small attempt to add to this collective body of work and portray a current cross-section of Jewish life in the Diaspora and in Israel, along with dishes that tell their own tale of family and culture. Some of the communities portrayed in the book are large and expanding; others are small and determined to flourish against the odds; some are relatively new and others venerable; some intrigued me because of their geographical location, others because of their history; and there are individual stories that may make for uncomfortable reading. Yet, we cannot understand why and what we are today, without understanding the past which brought us here.

So, this book comes with a qualification. Or maybe several. First, this is not a definitive compendium of Jewish recipes. Those included are but a small sample of a vast repertoire; sadly, because of space, many classic and favorite recipes have had to be left out, many communities unrepresented, many tales left untold. However, I hope that those unfamiliar with Jewish cooking will learn that it is more than corned beef on rye, and that both the Jewish and non-Jewish reader will find something new, informative – and tempting. A little *forspeise* (appetizer) of the pleasures of the Jewish table. I hope, also, my own Ashkenazi roots have not unduly influenced my view of the Jewish kitchen, as for me this book, too, has been a journey of discovery.

Secondly, in the kosher Jewish home, there are meat meals or dairy meals, and while individual recipes can, of course, stand perfectly well on their own, without this frame of reference they are like Friday night without the candles, kiddush without the wine.

Thirdly, I learned a long time ago that if you take two Jewish cooks, you end up with three opinions, if not thirty. So, if these pages do not correspond to your view of how to make the perfect latke or lentil soup, all I can say is it is part of a great Jewish tradition to argue about everything in life, including the size of the chopped onion.

Finally, there is one ingredient that no home should be without, and no cook should leave out of the recipe. It's the one thing that made my mother's Jewish cooking so special for me. Love. Lots of love. Whether or not you cut the ends off the brisket.

Clarissa Hyman

Food and festivals

THE DIETARY LAWS OF KASHRUT

Ever since Adam and Eve were warned not to eat the fruit of the Tree of Life, Jews have been required to be disciplined in matters of the table, guided by the dietary laws of Kashrut.

Kosher means "fit to eat," and one of the central restrictions is the separation of milk from meat. This derives from Moses's thrice-repeated warning not to seethe a kid in its mother's milk. As a result, kosher homes keep different sets of knives, pots and cooking utensils for dairy and meat meals (plus two extra sets for Passover use only). In addition, the Code of Jewish Law requires that a certain length of time must elapse between the consumption of milk and meat products.

Four-legged animals must have cloven hooves and chew the cud, so goats, sheep and cattle are permitted, but not pigs. Venison can also be eaten in theory, but deer shot in the open field cannot be slaughtered according to Jewish law. The most commonly eaten birds are chicken, duck, goose and turkey, but pigeon, pheasant and partridge are also permitted because the Torah only lists those birds which are forbidden to eat. All kosher meat and poultry must be prepared by the method of *shechitah* – a single, swift cut with an extremely sharp knife – which is believed to be the most painless way of slaughtering an animal. After shechitah, the animal must be thoroughly inspected to check it is without blemish. Most Jewish communities avoid eating certain animal fats and the meat from the hindquarters; only skilled butchers are able to remove the sciatic nerve where Jacob was wounded in his wrestling match with the angel. Finally, all meat must be soaked, salted and drained before consumption – blood, which is seen as the central life source, is forbidden by the Torah.

The Jewish kitchen contains a wealth of fish dishes – a particularly important religious symbol – but to comply with kosher requirements, fish must have fins and easily detached scales. Among the fish which fail this test are sturgeon (and caviar), all shellfish, eel, shark, monkfish and catfish.

Food that is neither dairy nor meat, is called pareve (also known as parev, or parve), and can be eaten with both categories. Bread is always deemed pareve, as long as it is made without butter or milk. Traditionally, fish and meat are not eaten together within one dish (using anchovies on beef, for example), simply because the Talmudic Rabbis regarded it as an unhealthy practice. However, it is acceptable to eat fish before meat – gefilte fish before roast chicken, for example – although it is often customary to cleanse the palate with bread and drink between courses.

In addition, there are rules on the cleansing of fruit and vegetables, and the supervision of milk, cheese and wine production. Kosher food technologists now regularly inspect thousands of processed products to ensure they do not derive from a non-kosher source. They will then either award them a rabbinical seal of supervision or approve their use by kosher consumers.

NOTE: This is a highly simplified overview of an elaborate code of regulations. As details of interpretation and practice can vary, anyone wishing further information should consult their own rabbinical authority.

"Jews have always talked a lot about food, partly because dietary prohibitions intensify the pleasure of the permitted."

CLOCKWISE FROM TOP CENTER:
THE ENTRANCE TO THE JEWISH
CEMETERY IN LODZ, POLAND;
MIAMI SYNAGOGUE; PURIM
FESTIVITIES IN JERUSALEM;
SABBATH IN ISRAEL; NEW YEAR
IN TRONDHEIM, NORWAY

THE SABBATH

The holiest day of the week sees a transformation in the Jewish household. Every Friday night, tables are laid with the best linen and china, aromatic smells steal out of the kitchen, and candles, lit to welcome the Sabbath, seem to burn with a special glow. It is a time when a family counts its blessings and blesses its children.

Before the Friday night meal, kiddush is recited over a goblet of wine in order to sanctify the start of the Sabbath. Prayers of thanks to God for giving us food from the earth are also made over two enriched and braided challah breads. They are covered with a white embroidered cloth that represent the dew that coated the manna during the Exodus. Before the bread is baked, a small piece of dough is always separated and burned in the oven; this ancient tradition, from which the bread takes its name, symbolizes the dough given to the priests at the time of the Temple. Challah is not, in fact, considered kosher without this ritual, and the salt in which the bread is dipped before it is eaten, recalls the salt on the sacrificial altar.

All at the table share in the wine and bread before eating the Friday night meal. The classic format for Ashkenazi Jews is chopped liver, chicken soup and roast chicken, but traditions vary enormously around the world. However, whether it is fish with chickpeas and cilantro, stuffed vegetables, brisket or chicken and rice, all the cooking and baking must be finished before dusk, and for the most observant, food needs to be prepared in advance for the next day, as no fire can be kindled on the day of rest. A great variety of special foods such as Ashkenazi cholent and Sephardi dafina, which can be kept hot, and cold fish dishes and vegetable salads, therefore, have evolved to provide food for the three mandatory meals of the Sabbath.

At the close of the Sabbath, at nightfall, a special havdalah ceremony with candle, wine and spices, takes place to say farewell to the "Sabbath Queen." It separates a day out of time from the rest of the week, the holy from the profane.

THE DAYS OF AWE: ROSH HASHANAH TO YOM KIPPUR

Rosh Hashanah, the New Year, is signified by the blowing of the shofar, the piercing call of a ram's horn that marks the ten-day period of introspection and contrition leading up to the fast of Yom Kippur, the Day of Atonement.

It is during these Days of Awe that divine judgement is said to be made on each person's life, yet this is also a time for feasting and family gatherings. Customs are numerous, but almost universal is the eating of sweet foods, to wish for a sweet year ahead: apples and challah dipped into honey; savory-sweet dishes such as tzimmes; moist, rich lekach or honey cake.

In many Sephardi and Mizrahi communities, a whole fish complete with head is served as a wish that the Jewish nation should be at the head of the nations of the world. Fish is also a symbol of fertility and a reference to the Leviathan. Leeks and beets represent luck over one's enemies; black-eyed peas a fruitful year; pumpkins so the family may "grow in fullness of blessing"; carrots because they are sweet, resemble gold coins when sliced, and, in Yiddish, wordplay means an increase of one's merits.

Challah breads are shaped into rounds to represent a wholesome year, the shape echoed in Syrian anise biscuits sprinkled with sesame seeds that symbolize good deeds in the year to come. Both stuffed kibbe and stuffed kreplach, represent the hope that divine but "hidden" compassion will "cover" both family and people throughout the year.

Dates are popular because they are sweet, symbolic of peace and the Hebrew word sounds like part of the prayers of penitence. A new, seasonal fruit is also eaten, along with a prayer that emphasizes the appreciation of new experiences. Pomegranates are prized because they stand for the hope that as many worthy deeds may be performed in the coming year as there are seeds. Some communities choose white foods for purity, or avoid the sour, bitter and black.

On the eve of Yom Kippur, it is deemed important to eat well – to heighten the contrast. The meal varies from the steamed coconut and saffron rice of the Bene Israel to the sweet and spicy breads of North African Jews, but chicken is the most usual choice. At the end, a little bread and a few sips of water are taken as symbolic food for the day ahead. Twenty-five food-and-drinkless hours later, many Ashkenazi break their fast with pickled or smoked fish to help restore the body salts lost during the day; others will take hot tea, fruit juice, almond or melon seed milk. In Curaçao they drink coffee topped with foamy, sweetened egg yolks; Persians sip grated apple with rosewater; Russian Jews eat spicy cinnamon buns; Greek Jews will have egg and lemon soup followed by fish or chicken. Libyan Jews may have chicken soup, spicy Libyan fish and semolina cake with honey syrup. Balkan and Middle Eastern Jews often eat lamb to recall the story of Abraham and Isaac.

SUKKOT

Immediately after Yom Kippur, there is a flurry of building and decoration work in observant Jewish homes to construct a temporary, open booth called a *sukkah*. For the seven day festive holiday, meals are taken here under a trellised roof that is open to the stars, yet partly covered with foliage to provide daytime shade.

Sukkot or Tabernacles recalls one of the three pilgrimages the Jews made yearly to the Temple in Jerusalem, as well as the temporary dwellings of the Israelites in the desert after the Exodus. As it falls at harvest time, it is also an agricultural festival of thanksgiving, with the sukkah adorned with seasonal flowers, fruit and vegetables. During this time, blessings are said over 'Four Species' of plants that are held, among other things, to symbolize particular virtues and characteristics of all the people said to make up a Jewish community: the *esrog* (citron), considered the "fruit of the goodly tree," and the *lulav*, a bunch of willow, palm and myrtle branches.

Both sweet and savory stuffed foods – strudels, *kreplach* (ravioli with a meat stuffing) and stuffed cabbage, onions, peppers, eggplants and so on – are eaten to emphasize the celebratory and abundant nature of the festival. On the last day, Hoshanah Rabbah, the day when the divine decree of Yom Kippur is finally delivered, many eat stuffed foods in order to allude to the "hidden" verdict. One mystical tradition says the red of the kreplach filling (linked to *din* – judgement) should be completely encased by the white pastry (linked to *chesed* – mercy), so that the outcome of the day be likewise.

The festival period ends on Simhat Torah, the "Rejoicing in the Law." In the synagogue, the last verses of the Five Books of Moses are read, and the cycle for the year begins again at Genesis; the scrolls are paraded and there is a great deal of singing and dancing. Foods are spicy and sweet, rich with fruit and nuts, sometimes arranged on a plate to represent the two furled scrolls of each Torah.

HANUKKAH

The word, in Hebrew, means "dedication," and this secular festival commemorates the post-biblical victory of the Maccabees over Antiochus and the re-dedication of the Temple in Jerusalem. According to tradition, only enough pure oil could be found to burn in the sacred *menorah* (candelabrum) for one day; miraculously this small amount continued to burn for eight days and nights. Ever since, in the Festival of Lights, Jews all over the world light candles or burn small cups of oil each night and eat a wide variety of foods fried in oil: latkes, doughnuts and fritters dipped in honey syrup. Dairy dishes are also eaten in memory of the Jewish heroine Judith, whose bravery is said to have inspired the victors.

Moroccan and Turkish Jewish communities also have special meals and gatherings on the sixth (the New Moon) and last nights of Hanukkah, respectively, but one of the most colorful

traditions used to take place in Russia. In the Flaming Tea Ceremony, glasses of tea were served along with brandy and large sugar lumps. The sugar was dipped into the alcohol, then placed on a spoon. As the lights were dimmed, the sugar was set alight with a taper passed from person to person, and the flaming cubes dropped into the waiting glasses.

TU B'SHEVAT

A minor festival, the name refers to the New Year of the Trees, a time in Israel at the beginning of the secular year when the sap starts to flow in the fruit trees. It has become customary to eat the fruits and nuts of biblical Israel, such as almonds, figs, dates, grapes, citrus and pomegranate, either fresh or dried. Some Sephardi communities call the holiday *Las Frutas* (Feast of Fruits), and have dozens of different varieties on offer throughout the day. A ritual meal tastes foods in categories of ascending spirituality.

PURIM

A time for carnivals, masquerade parties and general fun and games in the Jewish world, Purim celebrates the story of how Queen Esther saved her people when she triumphed over the evil minister Haman at the court of King Ahasuerus. A rare day off from restraint, it is the only occasion when Jewish people are actually encouraged to drink, until they are unable to tell the difference between the names of Mordecai and Haman.

The most traditional specialities are edible reference to the Purim story, such as Ashkenazi *hamantaschen* (triangular cakes, often with a poppy seed filling, that mock the shape of Haman's ears, pockets or three-cornered hat), and Sephardi *orejas de haman* (deep-fried pastry "ears"). Turkey is also eaten, because it represents the foolish King. Sweet and sour dishes are made in order to recall the grief that turned to joy when the tables were turned on Haman. Vegetarian dishes, especially ones with pulses and seeds, make the point that Esther would not eat meat when she lived in the royal palace. Kasha varnishkes, made from onions, kasha and bowtie noodles, is popular with Ashkenazi Jews; while date-filled pastries and marzipan petit fours adorn every table in Middle Eastern and North African Jewish homes.

Purim is also a time for charity and *shalah manot*, the exchange of carefully prepared and elegantly displayed gifts of fruit, cakes and cookies.

PESACH (PASSOVER)

Weeks before the festival arrives, the Jewish housewife metaphorically and literally rolls up her sleeves to engage in the mother of all spring-cleaning battles. Every observant home is subject to the most rigorous cleaning from top to bottom, inside and out, upside and down. Special sets of pots and pans are brought out for use, all non-Pesach foods disposed of, because no part of the house must contain a crumb of *hametz*, the tiniest speck of leavened matter, or prohibited cereal or grain.

Although it has its origins in two ancient nomadic and agricultural spring festivals, Pesach principally recalls the Exodus and the flight from slavery. For eight days, Jews are commanded to avoid all products that have been made with flour or leavening agents, and eat instead matzo, the "bread of affliction," a reminder of the haste in which the Israelites left Egypt. The festival of freedom, it starts with a Seder (Hebrew for "order"), a ceremonial family meal that is one of the most important of the Jewish year. It retells the story of the Exodus and is based on a liturgical text called the Haggadah. Symbolic foods are displayed and eaten, such as *maror*, a bitter herb, and *haroset*, a sweet dip made from fruit, nuts and wine that represents the clay used to make bricks.

Traditions, customs and religious obligations for Pesach are extremely widespread and diverse. Some communities, for example, will eat legumes and pulses and/or rice, others will not. The serving of lamb at the Seder also varies. Special dishes range from Egyptian coconut jam to Ashkenazi beet jam and carrot candy; Sephardi *huevos haminados* and savory matzo pies to Eastern European matzah brei; Greek and Turkish leek patties and fish in egg and lemon sauce to Moroccan tagines of lamb or chicken with prunes. Restricted to matzo and matzo meal (also used year-round in the Jewish kitchen), the prohibition against the use of wheat flour has been the stimulus for an amazingly creative range of recipes, too numerous to mention and a whole sub-category of Jewish cooking in itself.

Moroccan Jews, at the end of Pesach, celebrate a special holiday called Meenounah, when they freely visit friends and relatives, feasting on special foods such as *muflita*, thin wheat pancakes laden with butter and honey, and enjoy communal picnics the next day.

SHAVUOT (PENTECOST)

Originally the festival celebrated the start of the wheat harvest, but among the offerings taken to the Temple were the *bikurim* or first fruits, primarily barley, wheat, figs, grapes, pomegranates, olives and honey. However, it also became associated with the giving of the Law to the Jewish people at the Revelation at Mount Sinai, and the traditional food of Shavuot reflects these two themes.

Dairy produce is widely consumed, partly both because this is a time when milk production is at its height, but also for manifold symbolic and mystical reasons. White foods such as rice and milk are eaten, for example, because they signify the purity of the Torah: Italian and Romanian Jews make polenta and mamaliga, respectively, with white instead of yellow polenta. Cheesecakes, blintzes, bourekas and tortelli, cookies presented like the two tablets of the Ten Commandments, desserts fashioned in the form of Mount Sinai, *siete cielos* (Judeo-Spanish seven-tiered breads or cakes), cold sorrel or fruit soups are among the most popular of holiday foods, still eaten for Shavuot by Jewish people throughout the world.

Dairy

Bagel schmears | Salmon & corn chowder | Pickled cucumber soup | Baltic herring salad | Cafe Scheherazade borscht | Summer fruit borscht | Mina de maza | Huevos haminados | Matzah brei | Bumywelos | Venetian pumpkin risotto | Bolo di pampuna | Curaçao keshi yena | Michael Katz's sea bass in spicy orange sauce | Baked halibut with horseradish cream | Sotlach | Date & rice pudding | Classic cheesecake | Cheese blintzes | Hazelnut rugalach | Zwetschenkuchen | Bublanina | Hungarian sour cream & spice cake | North African coconut & orange cake | Boterkoek | Marmorkuchen | Ma'amoul | Basbousa | Kougelhopf | Eggplant & Feta salad | Borrekitas de merendjena

Bagel schmears

I am a purist when it comes to bagels: they should be crisp and glossy on the outside, soft but still satisfyingly chewy inside. You need to take a bite and be unsure who will be the winner. Beware the factory bagel. I want them hand-mixed with a little egg and ever so slightly sweet, hand-rolled, boiled and not over-baked, neither too large, puffy or doughy. I want them plain. I want them on Sunday mornings only, with coffee and the newspaper. I want them halved and topped with smoked salmon and cream cheese. But, sometimes, I go meshugge and make one of the following schmears (as it sounds – schmear on the bagel – what else could it mean?).

Avocado and egg

PER PERSON

flesh from 1 ripe avocado	2 scallions, finely chopped
1 hard-boiled egg, chopped	1 tbsp mayonnaise
juice of ½ lemon	salt and pepper

MASH all the ingredients together well and season to taste.

Cheese and dill

MAKES ABOUT 1 CUP

(How many bagels that covers	7 oz cream cheese
depends on whether you schmear	1 tbsp sour cream
thick or thin or just enough)	1 tbsp finely chopped dill
	2 tsp lemon juice
	salt and white pepper, to taste

WHIP the cream cheese and sour cream until smooth, then stir in the rest of the ingredients. Serve chilled.

Liptauer

MAKES ABOUT 1 CUP

¼ cup butter, softened	1 tbsp chopped capers
5 oz cream cheese	½ tsp German mustard
1 tbsp sour cream	(optional)
½ tsp caraway seeds	1 tbsp chopped chives
½ tsp paprika	salt

CREAM the butter until fluffy then beat in the cream cheese. Combine well then add the rest of the ingredients. Mix thoroughly and chill for at least 2 hours before serving.

A digression on the bagel

Jewish gourmet-philosophers have long pondered the question, which came first, the bagel or the hole? We are not just talking a roll with a hole, the bread equivalent of a Barbara Hepworth sculpture, but a symbol, an icon, a mystery, already. The origins of the bagel are unclear, but the word itself is said to derive from the Middle or High German verb *boygen* – to bend, linked to *bügel*, which means stirrup. A delicacy, because they were made of costly white flour, the bagel was supposed to be lucky because it represented the circle of life. According to John Cooper in *Eat and Be Satisfied*, it was first mentioned in the regulations of the Krakow community in 1610, which stated they could be sent as gifts to women about to give birth. Presumably you clamped one in your mouth to prevent yourself from screaming.

The bagel met its life partners, smoked salmon and cream cheese, in the New World. It has been suggested by anthropological analysts that salmon, a blood-like fish that bore a resemblance to ham, subtly challenged the dietary laws. Personally, I just think it was a marriage made in heaven. Which is why the egg and bacon bagel will always end in divorce.

"Food gives you an appetite, but an appetite does not give you food." JEWISH FOLK SAYING

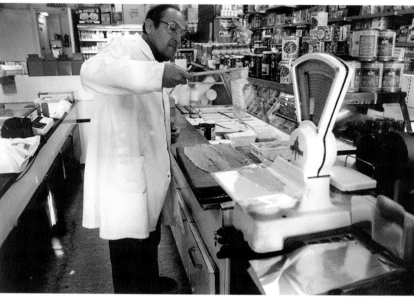

Salmon & corn chowder

A tribute to the "Frozen Chosen" communities of Alaska. Cold but committed, early Jewish pioneers were involved in trading, furs, shipping – and the Alaskan salmon industry.

SERVES 6

3 tbsp butter

1 onion, diced

6 celery sticks, diced (or 3 sticks and 1 leek, sliced)

1 red pepper, diced

1 tbsp all-purpose flour

8 oz new potatoes, cut into small pieces

2½ cups fish or vegetable stock

salt and pepper

1¼ cups whole milk

kernels from 2 husked ears of sweet corn or 3½ oz canned or frozen corn

1 lb skinned salmon fillet

⅞ cup crème fraîche or sour cream

1 oz parsley, finely chopped

MELT the butter in a large pot. Add the onion, celery, leek (if using) and red pepper. **COVER** and leave to soften over low heat.

STIR in the flour and cook for 1 minute, then add the potatoes, stock and seasonings. Bring to a boil then reduce the heat, cover and simmer until the potatoes are tender.

ADD the milk, sweet corn and salmon and simmer for 10 minutes, then stir in the crème fraîche or sour cream and parsley. Serve hot.

"Sabbath without fish is like a wedding without dancing."
JEWISH SAYING

LEFT TO RIGHT:
KOSHER DAIRY PRODUCTS;
LONDON DELI;
JOHANNESBURG DELI

Pickled cucumber soup

A recipe from Israeli-born Gaby Nonhoff, who now lives in Berlin where she runs Partyservice, a successful catering business. The soup is rather like a liquid German potato salad, but don't use saccharin-sweet pickles, half-sour, sweet-and-sour, or even sour-and-sweet ones. The intensity softens as it cooks, so the end result is pleasantly sharp but not mouth-puckering.

SERVES 4

2 lb 4 oz new potatoes
2 onions, finely chopped
¼ cup butter
2 quarts vegetable stock
  (or half stock and half water)

white pepper
can of sour, pickled Israeli
  cucumbers (110 oz drained
  weight), diced
⅞ cup sour cream
dill, chopped, as garnish

BOIL the potatoes until just cooked, then peel and dice.
SAUTÉ the onions in the butter until soft, then add the potatoes and stock. Season with pepper and simmer for about 20 minutes. Add the cucumbers and simmer for another 10 minutes.
POUR the sour cream into a mixing bowl and slowly mix in 1–2 ladlefuls of stock. Turn the heat down to very low and stir the sour cream mixture into the rest of the soup.
SPRINKLE dill over top, as a garnish, just before serving.

Baltic herring salad

A shtickle pickle is pure poetry – and it rhymes as well. A little pickle, be it herring, gherkin or beet, gives a person an appetite. Herrings, in particular, were once regular fare, so ubiquitous in Eastern Europe that to this day many an Ashkenazi Jew secretly believes that herring isn't fish, it's herring.

This herring salad probably started off life as a *forspeise*, something to kick-start the taste buds, the Yiddish equivalent of an *amuse-gueule*, but you could serve it as a main course with black or rye bread and butter. As for the sour cream – don't stint. Everything tastes better with sour cream.

SERVES 4–6

1 lb 2 oz jar pickled herrings or
  Matjes, drained
2–3 cooked beets, cubed
1 apple, cored and cubed
  and sprinkled with
  lemon juice

1–2 dill pickles, diced
2–3 tbsp sour cream
1 oz dill, finely chopped

CUT the pickled herrings into small pieces and just before serving arrange them in a dish with the beets, apple and pickles.
TOSS gently with the sour cream and dill.

Cafe Scheherazade

WHEN A HOLOCAUST SURVIVOR WAS ASKED BY A EUROPEAN OFFICIAL AFTER THE
WAR WHERE HE WANTED TO GO, THE SURVIVOR REPLIED, "AUSTRALIA." "SO FAR?" WAS
THE SURPRISED RESPONSE. THE MAN SIMPLY SHRUGGED HIS SHOULDERS AND
REPLIED, "SO FAR FROM WHERE?"

Life is as much about miracles as tragedy. It was a miracle how Avram and Masha Zeleznikow, both followers of the Bund, the revolutionary labor movement that turned thousands of Eastern European Jews into rebels and fighters, met each other. It was a miracle how they survived terrible, heart-breaking years of war chaos, deprivation and persecution, before finally arriving in Melbourne, where they opened what was to become the city's most famous Jewish restaurant. And it was also a small miracle of sorts how their son John met his wife, Lisa. The Jewish word is *beshert* – destined.

It all comes back to the Cafe Scheherazade. Just how it got its name is a tale of 1,001 nights, too long to be told in these pages, but the story is hauntingly and beautifully chronicled in the book of that name, a moving blend of fact and fiction, by Melbourne writer Arnold Zable, who traces the family's journey and that of other habitués of the restaurant – an epic tale that takes in fighting with partisans in the forests and swamps of Lithuania, the liquidation of the Vilna ghetto, imprisonment, perilous escapes, journeys, separations, a great love story and refugees who ran and ran until they finally came to rest in a bright new continent, in a great city at the very ends of the earth.

Records show that at least seven Jews arrived at Botany Bay with the first fleet in 1788. Like their non-Jewish fellow travelers, the early settlers were a mix of expelled convicts, free settlers and fortune-hunters. Melbourne's Hebrew congregation was founded in 1841, and the first synagogue built in 1847. There was a steady influx throughout the 20th century, many of whom lived in St. Kilda, but from a poor immigrant area the district slid further downmarket into one for backpackers and itinerants, pimps and prostitutes. The beachside neighborhood, however, is on its way back up. Animated and increasingly gentrified, the streets, bounded by the curving tracks of the local trams, hum with a lively buzz from the multitude of galleries, bistros, streetside cafés and spectacular cake shops. The Cafe Scheherazade has been an institution, a local landmark since 1958.

Masha and Avram's daughter-in-law, Lisa Zeleznikow, takes the family story into modern times, where destiny once again played its part. 'I had been working at the *Jewish News* in advertising, and I was asked to go down there and talk to them. That really excited me, the thought of all that free food! Over the most delicious schnitzel (one regular describes the restaurant as the *schnitzel Gan Eden*, the schnitzel garden of Eden!) I got chatting to Masha, who – can you believe this? – started to tell me about her son the professor and the single father! She asked if she could give him my phone number, so I owe everything to that chicken schnitzel!'

The restaurant remains a shrine to '50s retro, still with its sentimental can-can wallpaper and pretty, pastel-colored neon sign. The down-at-heel, derelicts, waifs and strays who once populated

SCHEHERAZADE RESTAURANT

35 YEARS IN ACLAND STREET

Noisy, crowded, familiar.
A place, like home,
in which to laugh and
gossip, argue and cry,
read, play cards.

CLOCKWISE FROM TOP CENTER:
AVRAM ZELEZNIKOW; THE CAFE
SCHEHERAZADE BOOK; THE
MELBOURNE SKYLINE; A CAKE
SHOP IN ST. KILDA; THE
CLOCKTOWER OF FLINDERS
STREET STATION, MELBOURNE

RIGHT: AVRAM AND
MASHA ZELEZNIKOW

the neighborhood have given way to a more sophisticated, albeit motley, crowd of students and artists, craftsmen and media folk, alongside the core of Holocaust survivors who were the restaurant's first customers. In this cafe of old-world dreams, there are those who still eat there every day, as they have been doing for nearly 50 years; one doughty group meet daily for coffee at 9 a.m. Their lives have seen too much change. Although Melbourne now has more than 45,000 Jewish inhabitants, the largest number of any Australian city, the cafe remains a small refuge where time and decor stand comfortingly still. Noisy, crowded, familiar. A place, like home, in which to laugh and gossip, argue and cry, read, play cards. A place in which to both remember and forget impossible, terrible memories.

Pumpkin soup and pavlova have become Australian-Jewish New World staples, but at the Cafe Scheherazade the menu remains an encomium to Old World tastes. Nothing has changed, even down to the terrible canned fruit salad (only family are allowed to say this, of course), but what does that matter when you've got the best baked cheesecake ever, apple cake and cheese blintzes as well as chicken soup and knaidlach, braised brisket, cabbage rolls, borscht... It's a menu every customer can recite by heart like poetry, a poignant libretto.

Masha describes in a bittersweet tone how many of her recipes were based on those she learned from her mother. "In Poland, I studied medicine for three years until the day I was forced to flee. I always thought I would be a doctor. In Siberia, in the work camp, I worked in the communal kitchen and would dig potatoes with my hands at night from beneath the snow; later in Kazakhastan, we would steal beet from the local sugar mill, that my mother would make into soup. I would never have believed that one day I would have my own restaurant called Cafe Scheherazade and that I would end up teaching my mother's recipes to a Greek chef."

Following in the footsteps of a great *baleboste** mother-in-law is no easy matter. However, John, a professor of computer science, no longer gets excited about the thought of the Cafe Scheherazade roll-call, having grown up eating there day in day out, so Lisa tends, instead, to cook her own mother's recipes. "I was so excited when I first made lokshen pudding because it tasted so much like my mother's. It was so very comforting! My mother-in-law makes her gefilte fish the Polish way, quite sweet; but my family's way is more in the Litvak style, without sugar. Please don't get me wrong, I dearly love my mother-in-law and her food, but these recipes are special to me. My mother's mother was from Romania and her family emigrated to Manchester [England] in 1902. She came to Australia as a war widow when my mother was 18. So, I have my own memories and those recipes make me feel at home wherever in the world I may be living."

Masha and Avram are now retired and the restaurant is under new ownership – but they have an agreement they can eat there every day. Nu, where else should they go?

*Baleboste is Yiddish for female head of the house, owner of the business and/or a conscientious homemaker.

Cafe Scheherazade borscht

Beet soup was often the only meal of the day in Poland and Russia, the original Borscht Belt, so it was a test of the housewife's ingenuity to vary the routine. When the temperature plunged below zero, there would be steaming bowls of meat and cabbage borscht to keep frozen body and soul together; in summer, a cold dairy version, part soup, part drink, part smoothie, was universally popular. This refreshing, chilled borscht has been on the menu of the cafe ever since it opened.

SERVES 4

5 beets, peeled and cubed

2 quarts cold water

1 tbsp salt

½ cup sugar or less if preferred

½ cup lemon juice

1 cup plus 1 tbsp yogurt or sour cream, strained

PLACE the beets in a pan and cover with the water. Bring to a boil and add the salt and sugar.

COVER and simmer until the beets are soft. Remove from heat and let cool to room temperature.

STIR in the lemon juice. Fold in the yogurt or sour cream. Do this gently or it may curdle.

SERVE chilled in glasses.

You can also serve this soup with freshly fried latkes (see page 116), or with boiled potatoes with butter and dill.

"For borscht you don't need teeth."
JEWISH PROVERB

27

Summer fruit borscht
aka borscht without the beet

Cold fruit soups are extremely refreshing in the blistering heat of an Israeli summer and, according to Joan Nathan in *The Jewish Holiday Kitchen*, were brought to Palestine by immigrant German Jews in the early part of the 20th century. You can use different proportions of ripe fruit or just plums or cherries (sour if possible). Or use blueberries, red currants or peaches, depending on what is available. Adjust the sugar to taste, but the soup needs to be a little tart. Serve either as a dessert or as a first course in hot weather; just avoid waving your spoon as you talk and eat – the stains will never come out of that nice white shirt.

SERVES 4

1 lb 2 oz plums, halved and pitted

10 oz cherries, pitted

10 oz nectarines, halved and pitted

1 tbsp sugar (or more, depending on how sweet the fruit is)

2 tbsp lemon juice (or less, ditto)

2 long strips lemon or orange zest

pinch of salt

1 cinnamon stick

4 whole cloves

1¼ cups red wine

1¼ cups water

1 tsp cornstarch

sour cream, to serve

lemon slices or mint sprigs, to garnish

PLACE the fruit in a saucepan with the sugar, lemon juice, zest, salt, cinnamon stick and cloves. Pour in the wine and water and bring to a boil, stirring occasionally.

REDUCE the heat to low, cover and cook for 10 minutes or so until the fruit is tender.

FISH out the cinnamon stick and cloves, then push the stewed fruit through a food mill (better than a blender as it also discards the skins). Return the purée to the pan.

MIX the cornstarch with 2 tbsp of the soup, then slowly stir into the fruit soup. Bring to a boil over high heat, stirring constantly.

LOWER the heat and cook until the soup thickens a bit.

TASTE and adjust the sugar/lemon ratio as required.

POUR into a serving bowl, set aside to cool, then chill for 2–3 hours before serving with sour cream. Top with either a wafer-thin slice of lemon or some mint leaves.

PASSOVER RECIPES

Mina de maza
Sephardi matzo pie

Serve with *huevos haminados* (slow-cooked eggs), symbols of the mystery of life, as well as the hope of life and the grief of death. And you thought an egg was just an egg…?

SERVES 4

14 oz fresh spinach

2 eggs

3½ oz Feta cheese, crumbled

3½ oz Kashkeval, Pecorino, or Parmesan cheese, grated

1 oz dill, finely chopped

salt and pepper

1 tbsp vegetable oil

5 sheets matzo

warm water

PREHEAT the oven to 350°F.

BRIEFLY steam the spinach until it just starts to wilt, drain well and roughly chop.

BEAT one of the eggs and mix with the spinach, both cheeses, dill, salt and pepper. Set aside.

BRUSH a 10x8-inch ovenproof dish with the oil to coat. Place in the oven to heat for a few minutes.

SOAK all the matzo in warm water briefly until soft and pliable but not mushy. Drain and pat dry on paper towel.

REMOVE the dish from the oven and cover the bottom with 1 sheet matzo and broken pieces of another matzo to fill the gaps.

SPREAD with the spinach filling, then cover with the remaining matzo.

BEAT the other egg and pour over the top of the pie.

BAKE for 45 minutes until the top is lightly browned, and serve warm.

Huevos haminados

Save a load of onion skins, then put them in a heavy pot along with some espresso coffee grounds and about a dozen eggs – you may as well do a lot while you're at it. Fill the pot with cold water and cook over a very low heat for hours and hours. Serve with mina de maza.

Matzah brei

Ashkenazi soul food.

SERVES 6

6 sheets matzo, broken into small pieces

6 eggs, beaten with salt and pepper

¼ cup butter

Soak the pieces of matzo briefly in boiling water until soft but still pliable. Drain well, pressing out excess water, and mix with the eggs. Melt the butter, and pour the eggs into the pan. Either scramble or make an omelet as preferred. That's it, folks.

Bumywelos

Matzo fritters from Salonika.

PER PERSON

1 sheet matzo

1 egg, beaten

salt

sugar, to taste

olive oil, for frying

honey, to serve

Soak the matzo in water, then squeeze out the liquid. Mash with the egg, salt and a little sugar. Fry tablespoons of the mixture in olive oil until brown on both sides and serve drizzled with honey.

RIGHT: MINA DE MAZA

Venetian pumpkin risotto
Risotto di zucca

The Venice Ghetto has embraced – or enclosed – the community for nearly 500 years. In 1516, the city was the first to segregate Jews behind high walls, locked at night, a template that would be replicated through Europe. The word *ghetto*, in fact, derives from the Venetian dialect term for the foundries where the district was established. At its height in the 17th century, the bustling, cosmopolitan Ghetto, home to over 4,000 Jews, had become a center for Jewish scholarship, culture and commerce. The then Rabbi of Venice even decreed that travel by gondola was permitted on the Sabbath. Numbers, however, had fallen to around 1,500 by the time the World War II broke out. The Ghetto was physically undamaged. Only lives were shattered.

Today, the dwindling community now numbers around 400, but still supports a range of educational, cultural and charitable activities, as well as a fine, small Jewish Museum. Services take place in various of the five Renaissance and Baroque synagogues, adorned with rare marbles, antique wood and rich fabrics in exquisite designs that reflect the origins of their founders: the Italkim (native Italian Jews who have been in Italy since the 2nd century B.C.), the German Ashkenazi majority, the learned Levantine Jews and the wealthy Portuguese. Jewish tradition dictates there should be nothing between a house of prayer and the sky above, between man and God: limited space in the Ghetto meant the *scole* (schools) were built like attics, concealed on the upper floors of the tightly-packed, high-rise buildings surrounded by a filigree network of narrow canals, passageways and bridges.

Distinctive Jewish-Venetian dishes include spinach stalks braised with oil, garlic and vinegar; sardines or sole in *saor*, marinated in vinegar with onions, pine nuts, and raisins; rice with raisins; goose breast stewed with tomato and garlic; and zucca, the "blessed" golden pumpkin of the Veneto, loved for its color of prosperity and, according to Joyce Goldstein in *Cucina Ebraica*, also for the resonance of the words *zucca barucca* with the Hebrew *baruch* or "blessed."

Risotti are made with all the vegetables of the Rialto market, but Claudia Roden quotes Giuseppe Maffioli, author of *La Cucina Veneziana*, who says the technique used in the Ghetto was to add the liquid in one go, as in an oriental pilaf, rather than gradually stirring it in to the rice. It seems to break the rules, but works beautifully when made with Vialone Nano, the traditional rice of the Veneto.

SERVES 4

2 tbsp olive oil

4 sage leaves, finely chopped (plus extra leaves, if desired, to garnish)

1 large garlic clove, finely chopped

1 lb 2 oz pumpkin or butternut squash flesh, cubed

salt and black pepper

3⅓ cups Vialone Nano rice

½ cup white wine

1 quart hot vegetable stock

6 tbsp freshly grated Parmesan cheese

HEAT the oil and gently sauté the sage and garlic. When the aroma starts to rise, add the pumpkin or squash. Add a little salt and pepper and sauté for a few minutes.

SPRINKLE in the rice and stir for another minute. Add the white wine and cook for another few minutes until it evaporates.

POUR the stock into the pan, stir it around, then bring to a boil.

COVER and simmer until the squash is soft and the rice is cooked (about 20–30 minutes). The risotto should be quite moist.

JUST before serving, stir in the Parmesan and some extra black pepper. Top each portion, if you like, with a sage leaf or two.

FAR LEFT: WILLEMSTAD, CURAÇAO; LEFT: PUMPKINS

Bolo di pampuna
Pumpkin pudding from Curaçao

SERVES 10–12

2 lb 4 oz pumpkin or butternut squash, unpeeled weight

¾ cup butter

1½ cups sugar

4 eggs

⅔ cup milk or orange juice

1 tsp vanilla extract

1 tsp cinnamon (or more, to taste)

1 cup all-purpose flour, sifted

½ tsp salt

2 tsp baking powder

PREHEAT the oven to 350°F.

BOIL the pumpkin, mash and set aside.

CREAM the butter and sugar, then beat in the eggs one at a time.

MIX the pumpkin with the milk or orange juice, vanilla extract and cinnamon, then add to the creamed mixture. Blend in the flour, salt and baking powder and mix well.

POUR into a well-greased Bundt pan (10 x 3 inches).

BAKE for 1½ hours or until a skewer comes out clean. Cool in the pan before turning out.

"La verdad va enriva como la aceite."
– Truth rises to the surface like olive oil. LADINO PROVERB

Curaçao keshi yena
Stuffed Edam cheese

From *Recipes from the Jewish Kitchens of Curaçao* (see page 74). The term is in Papamiento, the native island language, and the recipe has been adapted to use fish instead of meat with the cheese. This is spectacular when served in the shell of a whole, scooped-out Edam, but you can use sliced cheese to line a baking dish instead. The recipe can also be easily halved. The ingredient list may sound curious but the flavors blend surprisingly well. In Curaçao it is often served with *bolo di pampuna* (which also works very well on its own as a dessert served with coconut sorbet).

SERVES 10–12

2 lb 4 oz Edam cheese, thinly sliced
3 tomatoes, skinned and chopped
2 onions, sliced
1 small clove garlic
1 green pepper, chopped
1½ oz sliced green olives
1 tbsp capers
¼ chili pepper, finely chopped, or Tabasco sauce, to taste
1 tbsp parsley
½ cup raisins and chopped prunes
1 tbsp tomato paste
2 tsp Worcestershire sauce
2 tbsp ketchup
2 tbsp piccalilli
salt and pepper
2 lb 4 oz tuna or salmon, cubed
butter, margarine or oil
5 eggs

PREHEAT the oven to 350°F.

LINE two deep, buttered baking dishes, each about 14 x 10 inches, with about two thirds of the cheese slices, overlapping the edges. Alternatively, you can use one very large dish or a handful of ramekins.

SAUTÉ the remaining ingredients, except the eggs, in the butter, then lower the heat and simmer for about 20 minutes until the tomatoes reduce. Beat 4 of the eggs and blend them into the vegetable mixture.

FILL the cheese with the vegetable mixture, and cover with the rest of the cheese slices. Lightly beat the remaining egg and spread over the top to seal. Place each dish in another slightly larger baking pan half-filled with boiling water, and carry carefully to the oven.

BAKE for 1½ hours until the mixture feels fairly firm to the touch. Either serve hot from the dish or allow to cool for 5 minutes and turn out onto a serving plate.

Michael Katz's sea bass in spicy orange sauce

Although now London-based, Michael Katz made his name with his highly acclaimed Jerusalem restaurant, Michael Andrew, overlooking the Western Wall. This recipe, he says, features the oranges for which Israel is famous and the spices brought with them by immigrant Jews from the Arab countries.

SERVES 4

6–8 oz sea bass (or salmon or cod) per person
salt and pepper
olive oil, for brushing
1 leek, cut into strips or circles
4 carrots, cut into fine strips or circles, or 8 whole baby carrots
12 sugar snap peas (or green beans)
4 scallions, trimmed
2 tbsp butter
1 tbsp chopped chives, to garnish

SAUCE

juice of 6 oranges
1 star anise or ½ tsp anise seeds
seeds from 3 cardamom pods
2 cloves
2 crushed black peppercorns
1 tsp grated fresh ginger or ½ tsp ground ginger
2 shallots, chopped
¼ cup white wine
½ tbsp sugar (optional)
6 tbsp butter, cut into cubes and kept in iced water

MAKE the sauce by gently heating the orange juice, spices, shallots and white wine until reduced by half. Strain, return to the pan and check the seasoning. Add the sugar, if desired, depending on the sweetness of the oranges. Set aside. (The sauce can be made up to 2 days in advance.)

SEASON the fish on both sides, lightly brush with olive oil and either grill or pan-fry for 4–5 minutes on each side.

GENTLY reheat the orange sauce, keep the heat low and gradually whisk in the cubed butter. Keep warm while you boil the vegetables in salted water until tender. Drain and toss in a little butter, then distribute between 4 serving plates or deep dishes.

DRIZZLE with orange sauce, top with a piece of fish and sprinkle with chives before serving.

Northern Lights

GALUT IS THE HEBREW WORD FOR "EXILE FROM THE HOLY LAND," AND OVER THE
CENTURIES THE DIASPORA HAS SCATTERED JEWS ACROSS THE GLOBE TO THE
FARTHEST OF FAR-FLUNG CORNERS. EAST, WEST, SOUTH – AND NORTH. AS FAR
NORTH AS A PERSON CAN GO, WHERE THE MYSTERIOUS NORDIC PLACE-NAMES ARE
FRAGMENTS FROM ANOTHER SAGA OF OLD, FORGOTTEN TIMES.

Outside Julius Paltiel's split-level modern apartment the world goes about its usual business; as the late summer light fades, shopkeepers close their shutters, the docks fall silent, and swarms of sensible Norwegian cyclists crisscross the broad, leafy streets of the city. Across the still, dark water of the achingly beautiful Trondheim Fjord the horizon stretches out toward the Arctic Circle, a single strip between heaven and sea.

Rosh Hashanah in Trondheim. Together with Jews all over the world, we light candles and make blessings over the traditional round challah breads baked that morning by Vera Komissar, Julius's wife. We dip apples into honey, symbols of hope that life will be sweet in the coming year. For Julius, however, surrounded by his children and grandchildren, each year the prayers have extra significance. It is another year in which to bear witness, honor the past and rebuild this tiny Jewish community.

Julius, community president, is a quiet spoken, modest man with twinkling eyes and a droll, *haimishe* sense of humor, but he is not a man with whom one easily argues. And if Julius also insists that Trondheim is the world's most northerly Jewish congregation then I, for one, am happy to believe it, despite the claims to a superior few degrees of longtitude from the more recently established community in Fairbanks, Alaska. Anyhow, what's a few miles here or there? And they can still point with pride to the fact they have the most northerly Jewish museum-cum-synagogue in the world.

There are some stories that are too terrible to tell and others so terrible they must be told. Julius Paltiel, Auschwitz survivor, has made it his life's work to tell both his story, and that of the other Jews of Trondheim.

Norway's original capital, over 1,000 years old, is circled by water, as if in a fairy-tale. The well-preserved wooden wharfs and warehouses, painted in soft Scandinavian colors like rows of overgrown beach huts, tell of a time when Trondheim flourished as a fishing, shipping and mercantile center.

Jewish traders began to arrive in the region in the 19th century, primarily from Denmark and Sweden, then from Russia and Eastern Europe, and subsequently spread even farther north with the building of the railway to the Arctic Circle. In 1851, they were officially accorded the right of settlement. Ever conscious of religious obligations and communal identity, in 1905 they founded a congregation and by 1920 had 326 members. In 1924, the former railway station was remodeled as a synagogue.

"Why not come back? It's very beautiful, a small town that feels like a big one."

CLOCKWISE FROM TOP
CENTER: WATERFRONT CAFES,
TRONDHEIM; CATCH OF THE
DAY; THE RIVER NID; TIMBER
WAREHOUSES; LOCAL
TRANSPORT; TRONDHEIM
SYNAGOGUE

LEFT: A NORWEGIAN FJORD

This small Jewish world was smashed to pieces with the Nazi invasion of Norway. Although some escaped to neutral Sweden, half the community were sent to the Falstad concentration camp, then on to almost certain death in Auschwitz. Only four – one of whom was Julius – returned from the camps.

The synagogue, which was used as a Nazi barracks, has been restored with reparation money from the Norwegian government. A dignified Wedgwood blue building with high arched windows, it faces the great Gothic Nidaros cathedral where Norwegian royalty is still crowned. The synagogue also houses a small museum, whose exhibits have been lovingly and carefully assembled: an installation of empty coat hangers; an insouciant 1928 wedding menu boasting "Fish Pudding" and "Fish à la Française." Nearby, there is a memorial in a quiet residential square to Cissi Klein, a 13-year-old schoolgirl pulled out of her class to be deported to Auschwitz. Drops of sadness in the sparkling Norwegian air.

Julius, however, is a proud figure in the synagogue. His grandfather was one of the community's founders, and he continues in the *shmatte* business, the family textile firm that was founded in 1891. He also tirelessly travels the country speaking on the Holocaust, accompanied by Danish-born Vera, who lectures on Jewish religion and culture. He has been the subject of a Norwegian television documentary, and Vera has written his biography *In Spite of Everything*, which not only documents how he was selected for the gas chamber six times and reprieved, but also how he was the subject of an appalling experiment by Dr. Mengele.

One of the last to leave Auschwitz on the Death March to Buchenwald on January 16, 1945, every date is etched in his memory, as deep and permanent as the names of all those who perished are engraved on the three sentinel memorial stones in the Jewish cemetery. When he talks about journeying to Hell and back, he is not referring to the hamlet of that name near Trondheim, so favored by postcard-senders.

After the war, 123 Jews returned to Trondheim and since then numbers have slowly increased; the community now runs a *cheder* (Hebrew school) and holds regular services. Unlike the rest of the Jewish world, however, who have to wait until three stars appear in the sky, this far north they fix their own timing to welcome in the Sabbath and festivals. Otherwise in summer the Sabbath would never come in, and in winter never go out.

It is an idiosyncratic approach but that, perhaps, is the way of small communities, where there is always an unspoken worry that there will never be enough to make a *minyan*, the ten men required for religious services. The restored synagogue, however, has brought new hope to Julius, who sees it as a positive focus for the renewal of communal life, and an influx of a few Russian and Israeli families has helped counter the loss of Trondheim's young Jews to the brighter lights of Oslo and beyond.

Shechita is not permitted in Norway, so kosher meat and other products have to be imported. Luckily, fish is plentiful, if expensive. Salmon, debased by ubiquitous farming, has become relegated to the second division; halibut remains the favorite festival fish and herring, of course. Multi-talented Vera has also written a Norwegian-Jewish cookbook, or rather a Jewish cookbook in Norwegian, *Jodiske Gleder*, featuring the Ashkenazi recipes that unify so many kitchens from Trondheim to Tel Aviv.

Julius's love of Trondheim and Norway is palpable. But the question remains, after his terrible wartime experience, why go back to a place where this could be permitted to happen?

In the classic Jewish way, he answers a question with a question, "Why not come back? It's very beautiful, a small town that feels like a big one. I was born here, and know there are good people here. Here I am part of an historic community, accepted as a person and as a Jew."

Baked halibut with horseradish cream

Vera makes this for Sukkot and other festivals. It's also good when made with salmon; even in Norway, halibut can be more expensive than meat.

SERVES 8

4 lb 8 oz piece of halibut,
    washed, dried and salted
1 egg
salt and pepper
matzo meal or dried, toasted
    breadcrumbs

butter
heavy cream
splash of white wine (optional)
lemon slices, to garnish

PREHEAT the oven to 425°F.

PLACE the halibut in a generously buttered, ovenproof dish.

BEAT the egg with some salt and pepper and pour over the fish, so it is thoroughly coated.

DREDGE the fish with matzo meal or breadcrumbs. Dot with lots of butter and bake in the oven.

AFTER 15 minutes, baste the fish with butter – keep basting as it cooks and add more butter as necessary. The crumbs should brown, but you may need to lower the heat if they seem to be browning too quickly.

BAKE for another 10–15 minutes then add a little more butter and some cream to the pan. Let the butter melt, then spoon a little over the fish. You can also add a splash of white wine. Lower the heat to 300°F and bake for 1–1½ hours.

GARNISH with lemon slices and take the whole dish to the table.

SERVE with horseradish cream (right), boiled potatoes and a green or cucumber salad.

Horseradish cream

1¼ cups whipping cream
1–2 tbsp grated horseradish

pinch of sugar
1–2 drops white wine vinegar

WHISK the cream until firm. Add the horseradish, sugar and white wine vinegar. Taste and add more vinegar, sugar or horseradish, as desired.

CHILL until ready to use. Don't make it too far in advance, a couple of hours at most.

Norwegian cucumber salad

MIX finely sliced cucumber with white wine vinegar, sugar, salt and white pepper to taste. Garnish with fresh dill or parsley.

"Don't rub your stomach while the fish is still in the pond." JEWISH PROVERB

Sotlach

This recipe is based on one given to me by Mary Alvo of Thessaloníki. She remembers her grandfather eating this traditional Judeo-Spanish milk pudding in alternate spoonfuls with eggplant pastele, but it is more usually served separately as a sweet or dessert, especially to break the Yom Kippur fast. The Turkish custom is to serve it as the first course of a wedding feast, to symbolize a sweet life. Another charming custom, the Sabbath desayuno or breakfast, is to stencil children's names or initials on top of the pudding in ground cinnamon. In the Balkans, it is sometimes topped with rose-petal jam.

SERVES 6–8

⅞ cup ground rice flour
6¼ cups whole milk
⅜ cup plus 1 tbsp sugar

CARAMEL

½ cup sugar
⅔ cup water

PREHEAT the oven to 325°F.

MAKE the caramel by dissolving the sugar in the water over low heat. Bring to a boil without stirring, then let it bubble away until the syrup turns amber – about 10 minutes. Pour into an ovenproof baking dish (10 x 8 inches). Set aside.

PUT the rice flour in a heavy-bottomed pan, and stir in a little of the milk to make a smooth paste, then stir in the rest.

HEAT at low heat and bring to a gentle boil, stirring steadily (don't be tempted to raise the heat or the mixture will catch and burn on the bottom).

WHEN it starts to thicken, add the sugar. Simmer for 5–10 minutes, still stirring.

WHEN the first small bubbles start to pop on the surface, turn the heat right down and simmer, still stirring, for another 5–10 minutes.

POUR the thick, creamy mixture over the caramel, and bake for about an hour or until the top develops a dried, wrinkled crust "like the skin of an old woman!"

SERVE either warm or chilled. (The pudding, which is quite soft and creamy when warm, will firm up once refrigerated, but should not feel rubbery.)

Date & rice pudding

White rice dishes to symbolize the purity of the Torah are popular at Shavuot among Jews of Middle Eastern origin, who also call the festival The Feast of the Roses. Many communities scatter petals on the holy scrolls, or sprinkle rosewater on the congregation during prayers. Accordingly, this sweet and delicate pudding is also flavored with rosewater – and honey to celebrate the Revelation at Mount Sinai and the arrival in "a land flowing with milk and honey."

SERVES 4

5 cups whole milk
½ cup short-grain rice
4 tbsp honey
½ cup slivered almonds
1 cup dates, pitted and chopped
2 tbsp butter
2 egg yolks
2 tbsp rosewater
crystallized rose petals, or ground cinnamon, to decorate (optional)

BRING the milk and rice to a boil, reduce the heat to very low and simmer for 1–1½ hours, stirring frequently, until the mixture becomes thick and creamy.

STIR in the honey, slivered almonds and dates. Simmer for another 20–30 minutes, stirring frequently. Stir in the butter until it is completely absorbed and remove the pan from the heat.

COOL slightly and beat in the egg yolks, one at a time. Finally, add the rosewater. Pour into a shallow serving dish and let cool.

SERVE the pudding either at room temperature or chilled, and decorate the top, if desired, with rose petals or ground cinnamon.

RIGHT: DATE & RICE PUDDING

Classic cheesecake

You can argue over whether cheesecake originated in Ancient Greece or the Middle East, but it was really adopted as a "Jewish" cake by the Jews of central and eastern Europe, who had access to a plentiful supply of cheese and cream, especially in early summer.

Shavuot is one of the three *shalosh regalim*, pilgrimage festivals, when, in ancient times, the devout would go on pilgrimage to the Holy Temple in Jerusalem. Although the festival is primarily linked to the giving of the Torah to the Jewish people, it also has agricultural origins in the onset of the wheat harvest. At Shavuot, the Book of Ruth, so evocative of pastoral life, is read in the synagogue, and dairy dishes are eaten at home. Cheesecake is, of course, no longer confined to Shavuot, but you have to agree that a religion that actually encourages you to eat cheesecake and blintzes can't be all bad.

This is one recipe among millions of contenders for the title.

	FILLING
1¼ cups all-purpose flour	1 lb 10 oz cream cheese
½ tsp baking powder	¾ cup superfine granulated
pinch of salt	sugar
⅜ cup plus 1 tbsp superfine	3 tbsp lemon juice
granulated sugar	½ cup cornstarch
6 tbsp chilled butter, cut into	4 tbsp raisins
small pieces	3 eggs, separated
1 whole egg	1 cup plus 1 tbsp sour cream
½ tsp vanilla extract	

SIFT the flour, baking powder and a pinch of salt, then add the sugar and butter and lightly rub in until it looks like breadcrumbs. Combine with the egg and vanilla extract. Mix into a smooth dough ball, cover and place in the fridge for an hour.

PREHEAT the oven to 350°F.

MAKE the filling by mixing the cream cheese with the sugar, lemon juice, cornstarch, raisins, egg yolks and sour cream. Whisk the egg whites until stiff, and fold evenly into the cream cheese mixture.

ROLL out the dough between 2 sheets of plastic wrap or parchment paper to fit the base of a 9-inch springform pan.

SPREAD the filling evenly over the pastry base and bake for 1¼ hours until pale gold and the edge of the cake feels firm to the touch. Turn off the oven, open the door (of the oven, not the back door) and let the cheesecake cool completely before removing.

Cheese blintzes

Although you can use other fillings, cheese blintzes are traditional among Ashkenazi Jews at the dairy festival of Shavuot, when the white of the cheese is said to represent the purity of the Mosaic Law. If two pancakes are folded into oblong shapes, rather than fans, and placed side by side, then they are said to resemble the scrolls of the law brought down from Sinai. As Leo Rosten pointed out in *The Joys of Yiddish*, blintzes are never referred to in the singular, probably because you never hear of anybody eating only one.

SERVES 4	FILLING
1 cup plus 2 tbsp all-purpose	2 lb 4 oz cream cheese
flour	4 tbsp sour cream, plus extra to
1 tbsp superfine granulated	serve
sugar	2 egg yolks
3 egg yolks	3 tbsp sugar
4 tbsp butter, melted	1 tsp vanilla extract
⅝ cup milk	pinch of salt
⅝ cup cold water	
vegetable oil, for frying	
butter, for frying	

SIFT the flour and sugar into a bowl. Make a well in the center, add the egg yolks and butter and slowly fold into the flour. Gradually add the milk and water and beat well until smooth. Strain, if necessary, to remove any lumps.

BETTER still, blend all the ingredients for 1 minute at high speed. Cover and refrigerate for a couple of hours or overnight.

MIX all the ingredients for the filling together and set aside.

GREASE a frying pan with a little oil and place over a medium heat. When the oil is very hot, remove the pan from the heat and pour 4 tablespoonfuls of batter into the pan center. Tilt in all directions (the pan, not you), to thinly spread out the batter. Put the pan back on the burner for 1 minute until the batter is just set. Shake to loosen the edge, then lift and turn the blintz with a palette knife or spatula (the toss and turn technique is not an officially recognized part of *The Jewish Kitchen*).

BROWN the reverse side of the blintz for about 30 seconds. Slide it onto an ovenproof plate and keep warm while making the rest.

SPREAD a generous amount of filling over each pancake, fold in half, then in half again to make fan shapes. Brown the blintzes in butter just before serving with (more!) sour cream or jam (and maybe a few berries for healthy eating).

Hazelnut rugalach

Rugalach (little twists) are like knishes – hugely popular in American-Jewish kitchens. Quite why this should be, I have not been able to find out, although Joan Nathan in *The Jewish Holiday Baker* explains that cream cheese was a New World addition to Austrian crescent-shaped *kipfel* pastries. Rugalach are eaten year-round, at Shavuot and also at Hanukkah in memory of the fatal small cakes Judith fed to Holofernes, which is why this melt-in-the-mouth hazelnut version is simply to die for.

MAKES 32 SMALL OR 16 LARGE

13 tbsp butter, softened

7 oz cream cheese

2 tsp superfine granulated
  sugar

2 cups all-purpose flour, sifted
  with a pinch of salt

¼ cup brown sugar

4 tbsp cocoa powder

2 tsp cinnamon

⅞ cup finely chopped hazelnuts
  (or walnuts)

2 tbsp butter, melted

1 egg white beaten with a
  little water

granulated sugar (optional)

CREAM the butter and cheese until well blended. Stir in the superfine sugar, then the flour and mix until the dough begins to hold together. Gather into a ball, wrap in plastic wrap and chill overnight.

PREHEAT the oven to 350°F.

COMBINE the brown sugar, cocoa, cinnamon and nuts and set aside.

CUT the dough ball in half and return one half to the fridge while you work with the other. On a lightly floured surface, roll out the pastry into a thin circle about 10 inches in diameter. The pastry may feel hard at first but it quickly softens. Use a cake pan or plate to help cut out a neat circle. Cut the dough circle into 16 or 8 equal pie-shaped wedges.

BRUSH the surface of the wedges with melted butter, then sprinkle evenly with half the nut mixture. Cover with a piece of plastic wrap and use a rolling pin to press the filling lightly down into the dough.

REMOVE the plastic wrap and roll up each wedge from the outside, wide end toward the point, so you end up with mini croissants. Place on a lightly greased baking sheet and brush with the beaten egg white. Sprinkle with a little sugar, if desired. Repeat with the remaining dough and bake for 20–30 minutes until golden brown.

LET cool slightly before transferring to a wire cooling rack.

Zwetschenkuchen
Plum flan

A German-Jewish cake for Rosh Hashanah. The name comes from *zwetsche* (or *quetsch*), a variety of small, dark blue plum found in southern Germany and Alsace that ripens in time for New Year and Yom Kippur.

1⅔ cup self-rising flour
pinch of salt
11 tbsp butter, chilled
½ cup superfine granulated sugar
zest of 1 small lemon
1 tsp cinnamon
1 small egg, lightly beaten

2 lb 4 oz damson (or Victoria) plums
½ cup toasted slivered almonds
confectioners' sugar, for sprinkling
sour or whipped cream, to serve

SIFT the flour and salt into a bowl. Cut in the cold butter and lightly rub the mixture with the tips of your fingers until it resembles coarse breadcrumbs. (If you have heavy hands, use a processor – grandma would have, if only they'd been invented.)

MIX in the sugar, zest and cinnamon. Bind the pastry with the egg, but as it should not be too moist, don't add it all at once. Chill for at least 1 hour.

MEANTIME, cut the plums in half and remove the pits. Depending on their ripeness, you may need to invoke several satisfying yiddish curses* if the pits refuse to come out easily.

PREHEAT the oven to 375°F.

GREASE a 10-inch flan pan with a removable bottom. Lightly press the pastry into the pan, covering the base and sides.

PACK the plums, cut-side down, into the pastry base. If preferred, cut them into quarters and arrange in an overlapping spiral. Bake for 50 minutes until the pastry is golden and the fruit soft and juicy.

LET cool in the pan. Sprinkle with the toasted almonds and some confectioners' sugar. Serve with sour or whipped cream.

*As in – "may you live to be 100 years and have a beautiful mansion full of beautiful bedrooms and never get a peaceful night's sleep in any of them."

Bublanina

Serve this Czech cherry sponge either with coffee and mountains of whipped cream or as a dessert with vanilla ice cream.

1 tsp butter
4 eggs, separated
½ cup plus 1 tbsp superfine granulated sugar
grated rind of 1 lemon
2–3 tsp lemon juice

½ tsp vanilla extract
pinch of salt
1 cup self-rising flour, sifted
10 oz fresh cherries, pitted and halved
whipped or ice cream, to serve

PREHEAT the oven to 350°F.

LIGHTLY grease a 9-inch springform cake pan with the butter.

WHISK the egg yolks until thick, then beat in the sugar, lemon rind, lemon juice and vanilla extract. Fold in the flour.

WHISK the egg whites with the salt until stiff, then fold into the egg and flour batter with a metal spoon. Finally, fold in the cherries.

POUR the cake mixture into the pan and bake for 45–50 minutes or until the cake is golden brown.

LET cool on a wire rack before removing from the pan.

LEFT: ZWETSCHENKUCHEN; ABOVE: BUBLANINA

Hungarian sour cream & spice cake

A cake of Hungarian origin, now much Americanized, rather like Zsa Zsa Gabor.

2 cups plus 2 tbsp all-purpose
   flour
1 tsp baking soda
1 tsp baking powder
4 tsp ground cinnamon
1 tsp ground cloves
½ tsp grated nutmeg

salt
⅞ cup chopped walnuts
1 cup plus 2 tbsp superfine
   granulated sugar
⅝ cup butter
2 large eggs
⅝ cup sour cream

PREHEAT the oven to 350°F.

SIFT the flour with the baking soda, baking powder, half the cinnamon, the other spices and a pinch of salt, three times. Yes, you read it right. This is an arm-aching, brain-numbing activity for which no machine has yet been invented. But grandma was right – it does help to aerate and lighten the cake in a way you can never achieve with a mix from a box. It also helps to tap the sieve on the edge of the bowl while whistling Bohemian Rhapsody.

MIX the walnuts with the rest of the cinnamon and ½ cup of the sugar. Set aside.

CREAM the butter with the rest of the sugar then thoroughly beat in one egg after the other. Mix in a bit of flour mixture, a bit of cream, a bit of flour and so on until all the flour and cream are incorporated.

LIGHTLY butter and flour an 8-inch springform cake pan.

POUR half the cake mixture into the pan then add two-thirds of the walnuts. Cover with the rest of the cake mixture and top with the remaining walnut mix.

BAKE for 50–60 minutes until gold and the cake slightly pulls away from the sides of the pan Leave in the pan for 10 minutes before turning out to cool on a wire rack. Bubbe would be proud of you.

"Hunger is the best spice of all." JEWISH SAYING

North African coconut & orange cake

As far as I can tell, coconut is one of the few nuts in the Jewish kitchen that has neither biblical nor religious significance, apart from its use in the coconut pyramid macaroons popular at Passover (Israelites, slaves, Egypt – get it?), but that is a question of form rather than content. In any case, I digress, and this Maghrebi cake drizzled with syrup is as luscious as the unknown role model for the Song of Songs. Serve with Turkish coffee and a glass of ice cold water, reclining on cushioned divans by tinkling fountains, wafted by the scent of orange blossom… Resist the urge to belly dance, however, after a slice too many.

1¾ cup desiccated coconut

⅞ cup freshly squeezed orange juice

1 cup plus 1 tbsp butter

¼ cup superfine granulated sugar

grated zest of 1 orange

4 eggs

2 cups plus 2 tbsp all-purpose flour, sifted with ¼ tsp

baking powder and 2 tsp cinnamon

1 cup ground almonds

⅓ cup sliced almonds

SYRUP

1 cup plus 2 tbsp superfine granulated sugar

⅞ cup freshly squeezed orange juice

PREHEAT the oven to 325°F.

GREASE and line a 9-inch springform cake pan.

SOAK the coconut in the orange juice for about 20 minutes.

BEAT the butter, sugar and grated zest until light and fluffy. Add the eggs, one at a time. Stir in the sifted flour, then add the coconut, juice and ground almonds.

POUR the mixture into the cake pan, sprinkle with sliced almonds and bake for 45–50 minutes, until golden. Ten minutes before the end of baking, make the syrup.

COMBINE the sugar and orange juice in a saucepan and stir over a low heat until the sugar dissolves. Raise the heat and boil, uncovered, for about 5 minutes until the syrup thickens.

POUR most of the hot syrup over the hot cake in the pan and let cool before turning out. Just before serving, drizzle the remaining syrup over the cake.

Boterkoek
Dutch butter cakes

Preserved ginger gives these much-loved, buttery pastries a distinctive Jewish flavor.

MAKES 18 SQUARES

2¼ cups butter

2 cups sugar

6 cups plus 2 tbsp all-purpose flour, sifted with a pinch of salt and 1 tsp ground ginger

2 tsp vanilla extract

12 oz jar of stem ginger, drained (reserve 2 tbsp syrup) and finely chopped

2 tbsp milk

PREHEAT the oven to 400°F. Generously butter a 9x12-inch baking pan.

CREAM the butter and sugar, then stir in the flour, vanilla and ginger (or combine in a processor). The mixture will have a rather crumbly, clay-like consistency, so pat and push into the baking pan.

MIX the reserved ginger syrup with the milk and brush over the mixture. Bake for about 25–30 minutes until light gold in color.

COOL for 5 minutes, then mark into squares. Let cool completely in the pan.

Marmorkuchen
Marble cake

Another deliciously old-fashioned German cake popular for Sabbath, or indeed any other time.

1¼ cups butter

1⅓ cups superfine granulated sugar, plus an extra 4 tsp

2 tsp vanilla extract

pinch of salt

5 eggs

3 cups all-purpose flour sifted with 4 tsp baking powder

6 tbsp milk

4 tsp cocoa powder

confectioners' sugar, for dusting

PREHEAT the oven to 350°F.

CREAM the butter and gradually beat in 1⅓ cups sugar, vanilla extract and a pinch of salt until the mixture is light and fluffy.

ADD the eggs, one at a time, then the flour and baking powder.

GRADUALLY beat in 2–3 tablespoons of the milk, but only as much as is needed to give a slow dropping consistency to the mixture.

POUR two-thirds of the batter into a greased 9-inch pan (you can use a round one, funnel or loaf shape – but whichever you use the batter should only fill three-quarters of the pan, as it will rise).

SIFT the cocoa and remaining sugar and add to the remaining third of batter along with 2–3 tablespoons milk, enough again to make a slow dropping consistency. Spread the chocolate mixture over the one in the pan, then lightly run a fork through them both, gently swirling the two colors together. (You are now permitted to lick the mixing bowl.)

BAKE for 50–60 minutes until the cake shrinks slightly from the sides of the pan. Let stand for 5 minutes before turning out. When cool, dust with confectioners' sugar.

RIGHT: MARMORKUCHEN

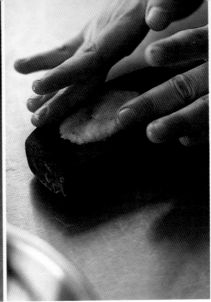

Ma'amoul

Middle Eastern pastries filled with dates and nuts

According to Gil Marks in *The World of Jewish Desserts*, these are one of the most ancient extant pastries. Made throughout the Middle East, there are many variations, both in dough and filling; the latter can feature walnuts, pistachios or dates, singly or in combination. Ma'amoul, or menena as they are sometimes called, are made throughout the year on all festive occasions. A surface design is imprinted by traditional wooden moulds or pincers; in *A Fistful of Lentils*, Jennifer Abadi describes the Syrian use of *maa'laat*, a tweezer-like instrument that pinches a design into the dough.

This recipe makes delicious pastries – or so I thought until I tasted ones made by some expert Sephardi cooks. And no, I can't tell you how they were different. It's not the ingredients, it's not necessarily the technique, but it's that special skill and lightness of touch that is only acquired through years of experience and generations of kitchen craft. But even my first attempt worked – and they're getting better all the time. I may not have a slender kibbe finger, but I'm on the way to mellah hips.

COMBINE the semolina, sugar and rosewater or orangeflower water. Heat the butter or margarine until it starts to foam then pour into the semolina and mix well.

HEAT the milk or water to just below boiling point, remove from heat and stir in the baking soda. Add to the semolina mixture.

MIX to a soft dough and knead lightly. Cover with plastic wrap and let sit for several hours.

PREHEAT the oven to 325°F.

MIX the ingredients for the filling together to make a softish paste.

PINCH off a piece of semolina dough, about the size of a large walnut, and roll into a ball. Place in your palm and gently cup your hand to push up the sides while simultaneously using your thumb (either hand!) to hollow out the dough. You should end up with a thimble or pot shape which you then fill with a teaspoon of stuffing. Mold the dough back over the top to seal the pastry and either keep as a pouch or roll into a ball again. (This all sounds much worse than it is in reality; it just needs time, a few tries and a positive attitude.)

IF you do not have a traditional mold, place the balls on a baking sheet, flatten slightly and use a fork to make a pattern on the surface.

BAKE for about 25 minutes. Do not allow to brown; they should just be lightly colored. Leave on the baking sheet to cool and firm up, then transfer to a wire rack or plate. Dust with confectioners' sugar.

MAKES ABOUT 48

6¼ cups fine semolina
½ cup superfine granulated
    sugar
2 tbsp rosewater or
    orangeflower water
1 cup plus 1 tbsp butter or
    margarine
1 cup milk or water
½ tsp baking soda
confectioners' sugar, for
    dusting

FILLING

1 cup Mejdool (semi-dried)
    dates
⅞ cup chopped pistachios or
    walnuts
2 tbsp rosewater or
    orangeflower water
1 tsp ground cinnamon or
    ground cardamom
2 tbsp superfine granulated
    sugar

Basbousa
Semolina and yogurt cakes

This is one of the most popular Middle Eastern sweets, with as many versions as there are tales in *1,001 Nights*. It is based on yogurt which, in one form or another, has been favored by all the ancient civilizations of the region. One apocryphal story links the discovery of yogurt to Noah: having nowhere to store the milk produced by all the creatures onboard, he used sewn-up bags of animal stomachs, and found one day the milk had curdled and thickened – a story, perhaps, not far from the nomadic truth.

In *The Best of Baghdad Cooking*, Daisy Inry describes how *leban* (homemade yogurt) was "usually made in round wooden boxes about 6 inches high and 12 inches in diameter. Women balancing tiers of boxes of leban on their heads – sometimes taller than the women themselves – are common sights in the streets of Baghdad."

In this recipe, semolina gives a slightly nutty, slightly crunchy texture, but you do need to use fine grain to avoid graininess.

7 tbsp unsalted butter,
  softened
¾ cup plus 1 tbsp superfine
  granulated sugar
2 eggs
3½ cups fine semolina
1 tsp baking powder
½ tsp baking soda
1 tsp cinnamon or vanilla
  extract
⅔ cup Greek yogurt
blanched almond halves,
  for decoration

SYRUP
2¼ cups sugar
1½ cups water
juice of 1 lemon
1 tbsp rosewater or
  orangeflower water

PREHEAT the oven to 350°F.

LIGHTLY grease an 8x12-inch shallow baking pan.

CREAM the butter and sugar and beat in the eggs, one at a time.

SIFT the semolina, baking powder, baking soda and cinnamon and stir into the butter mixture along with the yogurt. When the batter is smooth, pour into the baking pan and spread evenly.

CUT diagonal parallel lines through the cake in both directions to form diamond shapes (a ruler may help avoid wobbly lines). Place an almond in the center of each diamond.

BAKE for 35–40 minutes until firm and light brown.

PREPARE the syrup by first dissolving the sugar in the water over medium heat. Add the lemon juice and bring to a boil. Reduce the heat and boil gently for 10 minutes until the syrup thickens. Remove from the heat, stir in the flower water and set aside to cool.

POUR spoonfuls of syrup over the hot cake until it can absorb no more. Set aside to cool before serving.

"Honey in the mouth won't help bitterness in the heart." JEWISH PROVERB

Kougelhopf

The Jewish presence in Alsace, along the Rhine Valley, dates back a thousand years. The Romans are believed to have brought the secret of foie gras production with them when they occupied Alsace, but it was the Jewish community who specialized in the breeding of fat geese and kept the techniques alive long after the conquerors departed. The medieval Rhineland communities were also among the first to combine liver with onions and eggs – the homely chopped liver that later became the inspiration for pâté de foie gras. Or so the story goes.

Not surprisingly, the cuisine reflects both a strong French and German influence: dumplings and noodles, cheese and fruit tarts, cabbage and cinnamon. Conversely, a number of Alsatian dishes have taken on a Jewish character: carpe à la Juive, for example, is made with crumbled lebkuchen and wine vinegar to add a distinctive sweet-sour flavor to the sauce.

Choucroute garni is the main festive dish for all, adapted to use beef and goose fat instead of pork and lard. Likewise, bireweke, a spiced fruit bread made with dried pears, is a speciality for both Hanukkah and Christmas. Ripe, local pears are also poached, stuffed or used for a slow-baked, savory-sweet kugel made with onions.

A special brioche for Rosh Hashanah is stuffed with a rich almond cream, but kougelhopf, however, arguably takes place of honor on the Alsace Jewish table, and is traditionally eaten every Sabbath, as well as after Yom Kippur.

Kougelhopf should be made in the traditional 10-inch mold, but a Bundt pan or a 9½x3-inch fluted tube cake pan can be used instead.

⅞ cup slivered almonds
4¼ cups all-purpose flour, sifted with a pinch of salt
½ tbsp active dried yeast, reconstituted according to package instructions or ½ oz fresh yeast (always preferable for flavor)
½ tsp vanilla extract (optional)
¾ cup plus 1 tbsp superfine granulated sugar
⅞ cup lukewarm milk
1 cup butter
3 eggs
1 cup raisins, pre-soaked in water or, better still, Kirsch
confectioners' sugar, for dusting

GREASE the mold or cake pan and set aside. If desired, sprinkle some almonds over the inside of the mold.

PLACE the flour, yeast, vanilla extract and sugar in a bowl and mix well.

ADD the warm milk, butter, and eggs and beat for about 2 minutes, then add the raisins and remaining almonds and mix well to ensure that they are evenly distributed. Pour the mixture into the mold – it should fill about half the pan. Cover with plastic wrap and set aside in a warm place until the dough doubles in bulk.

PREHEAT the oven to 350°F.

REMOVE the plastic wrap and bake for 30–40 minutes or until a skewer inserted into the center comes out clean and the base of the cake sounds hollow when tapped. Cool in the pan for 30 minutes before turning out onto a wire rack. Serve dusted with confectioners' sugar.

"El tyenpo del kweshko dulse."

"THE TIME WHEN FRUIT STONES WERE SWEET." – LADINO FOLK SAYING FROM SALONIKA

On a soft summer night under a Balkan moon, we sit in the garden of an old Turkish house above the great Greek port and horseshoe Gulf of Thessaloníki. Far below, the lights from the multitude of fashionable bars and cafés, glossy shops and grid-like, grid-locked city boulevards shimmer with self-assured prosperity and sophistication. Thessaloníki, its plain-speaking natives proudly insist, was a fine, important place when that upstart of a capital, Athens, was a mere wretched village.

Yet, although industrious and hardworking, their sophistication is shot through with a kind of physical languor; a sensual haze seems to envelop Thessaloníki as it slips imperceptibly down the shore to meet the soft waters of the Aegean. It veins the city like drizzled honey on yogurt. But as we laugh, drink ouzo and eat dolmas, the scent of roasted eggplants drifts through the air, quickening the dark currents of the night, re-awakening the old voices. The memories of *El tyenpo del kweshko dulse*.

On July 11, 1942, the German occupying forces rounded up every male Jew aged 18 to 45 in Eleutherias (Liberty) Square, to be publicly humiliated and enrolled for forced labor. It was the beginning of the end for what was once the largest Jewish community in the world. Nearly 50,000 were deported and exterminated at Auschwitz-Birkenau, and virtually all evidence of Jewish life in the city was destroyed, including the immense 2,000-year-old cemetery.

Once upon a time, there was a Jewish city called Salonika. A powerful trading center at the crossroads of the Balkans, it was strategically sited on the great Roman road linking Italy and Constantinople (now Istanbul). Renowned for both religious learning and commercial influence, there had been Jews in the city since Roman times, artisans from Alexandria, but the pivotal historical moment came in 1492, when the Ottoman rulers encouraged large numbers of Sephardi Jews to settle here after their expulsion from Spain. Within a few decades 20,000 Spanish Jews, "the flower of Spain," joined the existing 2000 Greek-speaking "Romaniot" Jews of the city, eventually becoming the dominant group in terms of language, dress, manners and customs.

For nearly half a millennium their descendants formed the majority of the population; they gave an international stamp to the city, helping it become the second most important port in the Ottoman Empire. Yet Salonika also saw extraordinary reverses in its fortunes; over the centuries it would go from golden age to tarnished one, from wealth to economic decline, from a closed, rabbinical world to a secular, modern Western one. The golden age of the 16th century, when the city was famed for distinguished rabbis, its Talmudic academy, conservatory for religious singing and religious printing houses, would be followed by the coming of a false messiah, war and revolution, earthquake, fire and apocalypse.

By 1900, at the time of her second "renaissance," Salonika had approximately 80,000 Jewish souls out of a total population of 173,000: businessmen and bankers, weavers and woodcutters, merchants

… a sensual haze seems to envelop Thessaloníki as it slips imperceptibly down the shore to meet the soft waters of the Aegean.

CLOCKWISE FROM TOP CENTER:
THESSALONIKI SEA FRONT;
THE WHITE TOWER; CAFES IN
ARISTOTELOUS SQUARE;
THE SEA FRONT; THE PORT
OF THESSALONIKI

RIGHT: BAKER ALBERT
YEHUDA, THESSALONIKI, 1935;
OPPOSITE: EGGPLANTS

and civil servants, rabbis and firemen, porters and poets, peddlers and physicians, balladeers, scholars and mystics. Salonika was unique in the Diaspora in that Jews here enjoyed the freedom to engage in any job of their choice, including that of fisherman and stevedore. Indeed, such was the special character of the city that the port and docks fell silent on Saturdays.

There were Jewish shops, newspapers and publishing houses, clubs and social groups, numerous study houses and synagogues, many named after the places from which the first founders had originated: Castilia, Catalan, Aragon, Majorca, Lisbon, Sicilia, Calabria, Puglia, Provincia and more.

The system of communal welfare was highly developed, with free meals and grants to poor students, orphanages, a psychiatric asylum, a hospital, health centers and a home for the elderly, as well as dozens of schools and places of learning. After the Young Turks coup in 1908, both Zionist and socialist workers' movements flourished.

Judezmo-Ladino (Judeo-Spanish) remained the primary language of the streets, but Salonika was, in fact, one of the most cosmopolitan and vibrant cities in the world. The old Ladino-speaking world and culture, however, was already in decline: when the city became part of the modern Greek state in 1912, the ensuing population exchanges with Turkey and changing demographic, economic and social situation accelerated a trend of emigration to Israel, France and elsewhere. This was given even greater impetus by the great city fire of 1917, which destroyed most of the Jewish quarter.

The food of the Salonikan Jews also had its own distinct identity, a combination of dishes carried in folk memory from Spain, plus some drawn from the kitchens of their Turkish and Greek neighbors, and yet others unique to a city where the narrow, crowded streets were permeated with the scent of rosewater, caramelized onion, smoky grilled eggplant and ripe melons that floated out of every Jewish kitchen.

Today, on high days and holidays, the Jews of Thessaloníki still eat their traditional food. The kitchen is one of the few places where the Ladino language has survived, with the simple, unrefined dishes still described in the mother tongue. But, this ancient culinary heritage was almost extinguished by the Holocaust. Only those who survived could pass on their cooking lore. Fortunately, some of the extensive repertoire has now been chronicled in *A Taste of Sephardic Salonika* by Albert Arouh, based largely on the recipes of survivor Nina Benroubi.

"Salonikan Jewish food," he says, "is a lesson in simplicity. You need care and patience, of course, but it is the techniques that make it distinctive and full of flavor: stewing in oil, water and lemon; hot water pastry; the *batuta* of sautéed vegetables; a way of caramelizing onions three times to flavor a dish of white beans. And it needs little in the way of garlic, herbs and spices."

It was also a cuisine of poverty. "One hen would feed a family of four for two days, even the bones were ground into meatballs." Victoria Benuzilio told me, "Food needed to go a long way, so you would have small portions of many different dishes to add variety and richness to the table."

Daily dishes included stuffed vegetables, cheese or vegetable fritters, meatballs with walnut sauce, and chickpeas and beans in soup. *Taarinas* and *fideos* were thin homemade noodles, dried for several days in the sun; "*Azemos fideos*" was commonly used as an exhortation to be patient. Desserts still popular include *sotlach* (see page 40), *tupishti* (orange walnut cake) and *yaourtopita* (yogurt cake).

Vegetables predominate, with imaginative reworkings of a single type in half a dozen ways. Their beloved eggplant, for example, is rolled around ground meat, stuffed into pies, mashed

"Salonikan Jewish food," he says, "is a lesson in simplicity. You need care and patience, of course, but it is the techniques that make it distinctive and full of flavor…"

into salad with Feta cheese and oil, fried in a flour and ouzo batter or, above all, made into mouth-watering *borrekitas* (see page 60), the most emblematic Salonikan taste of home.

For Sabbath, no home would be without its slow-cooked meat *hamin* and *huevos haminados* (see page 30), but there would also be fried chicken balls; meatballs and plums; chicken broth with lemon and egg sauce; chicken necks with rice; wheat and roasted chestnuts. The *avdela* blessing, to see out the Sabbath, would be made over fragrant lemons, freshly ground coffee or cloves.

At the New Year, everyone became as round as their favorite coiled phyllo pies with spinach or cinnamon-flavored pumpkin. There were also leek fritters and fried small red mullet, preferred in Salonika to the large fish popular in other Sephardi communities, and always "eaten from the head down!" Albert recalls his mother saying, "You can give anything to the cats, except the head of the mullet!"

There were *bumywelos* (matzo fritters – see page 30), and chicken or lamb with peas, dill and spring onions for Passover; phyllo triangles with nuts and honey at Hanukkah; sesame seed sweetmeats for Purim. One unique tradition for the latter festival was the construction of detailed tableaux and figurines called *novyikas* made from sugar and water candy depicting scenes from the story of Queen Esther and wicked Haman. A few remarkably preserved examples are on show at the Jewish Museum, housed in one of the rare Jewish structures to survive the 1917 fire.

After the war, a tiny number of Jews made their way back. Their survival, in the camps, in hiding or fighting with the partisans, always a matter of chance. A twist of fate. Every Jewish family here has its story, but the few who returned did so for patriotic reasons: Greeks and Jews had fought together against the Nazis, and Thessaloníki was their home.

The post-war years were harsh but the Jewish community, which now numbers around 1,200, has rebuilt itself on the ashes of the past. While little remains of the old Jewish city – some splendid villas, the atmospheric Modiano market where one of the butchers' stalls supplies kosher meat – the impressive tradition of welfare support that always distinguished Jewish Salonika has been replicated. The community is small but active; there are three synagogues, a community center, a dignified and comfortable old age home, a primary school, Maccabee athletic club, and a summer youth camp. On Friday nights, they host communal dinners, and every fortnight the lively Ladino Society organizes *kavedjiko* evenings to celebrate the culture and language.

Looking to the future, president David Saltiel sees their potential as a new home and focal point for the remnants of other Balkan communities. "We want to be the center of Jewish life in Greece again; we are trying to keep our young people from moving away and also encouraging new families to move here from other countries in the world by assisting them financially, offering work, education and a full Jewish life. Although we are few in number, we have the will to keep our dream alive."

The Jews of Thessaloníki have not only spirit, but also resilience and pride in their Greco-Jewish identity. Whatever the odds, they are determined to honor the past, affirm the present and tell the truth to future generations.

Catharsis out of Hubris.

"That the generation to come might know them, Even the Children that should be born, Also should arise and tell them to their children."
PSALM 78:6

Eggplant & Feta salad

A recipe passed on to Victoria Benuzilio by her mother-in-law.

FOR 4 AS AN APPETIZER

Eggplants weighing approx
3 lb 5 oz
7 oz Feta cheese
2 tbsp extra virgin olive oil
(or to taste)

IDEALLY, you should grill the eggplants until black and blistered on the outside and soft and smoky inside, but you can also roast them in the hottest oven for about 45 minutes.

WHEN cool enough to handle, peel and press to remove excess liquid.

PLACE on a large plate or board and mash vigorously with a fork. (You can mash leisurely but it will take much longer).

WHEN the eggplant flesh is broken down, thoroughly mash in the crumbled cheese. Drizzle over the olive oil and mix to a smooth paste.

SERVE with pita bread and olives.

Borrekitas de merendjena
Eggplant pasties

Albert Arouh was born in Thessaloníki, but now lives in Athens where he works as a food writer. This recipe is from his book *A Taste of Sephardic Salonika*.

MAKES ABOUT 36
CRUST
1 cup corn oil
1 cup water
4¾ cups all-purpose flour
⅜ cup plus 1 tbsp yogurt
1 egg, beaten, for glazing

FILLING
2 eggplants
14 oz Feta cheese, crumbled
2 eggs
1 tbsp olive oil
salt and pepper

PREHEAT the oven to 350°F.

PLACE the oil in a saucepan with the water and bring to a boil. Remove from the heat and add to the flour and yogurt, mixing together well with a wooden spoon so it makes a firm pastry. Cool, cover and set aside while you prepare the filling.

ROAST or grill the eggplants. Set aside until cool enough to handle, then mash to a purée with a fork. Add the cheese, eggs, oil, salt and pepper and mix thoroughly.

KNEAD the dough until smooth and elastic. Pinch off pieces and press or roll into flat discs about 4 inches in diameter. Place a heaping teaspoon of filling in the center of each disc and fold the dough over to make a half-moon shape. Trim off the overhang of excess dough with the rim of a glass to stamp out neat parcels, and press down on the edges with your fingertips to seal well.

GATHER up the excess pastry and use for further pasties.

BRUSH the beaten egg over the surface of the pies.

ARRANGE on a lightly oiled baking sheet and bake for 50–60 minutes until golden brown.

"What is the Ladino for 'eat well'?" I asked. "There's no such expression," they answered, "Everyone always has a good appetite!"

RIGHT: BORREKITAS DE MERENDJENA

Meat

Chicken liver knishes | Chopped liver | Mushroom & barley soup | Lamb & lentil soup with cumin | Yemenite meat soup | Chicken soup | Zena Swerling's knaidlach | Mrs. Frazer's soup mandlen | Samuels family lokshen | Curaçao chicken soup | Bukharan plov | Bukharan carrot pilav | Georgian chicken | Moroccan chicken with dates | Green masala chicken curry | Persian jeweled rice with chicken | Cuban picadillo | Holishkes | Stuffed vegetables from Salonika | Stuffed onions| Keftes de prasah | Grandma Annie Friedman's sweet & sour meatballs | Iraqi beet kubba | Lahma bi ma'ala | Syrian rice & vermicelli | Baghdad beef with okra | Hungarian stuffed breast of veal | Lamalo lamb tagine with almonds & prunes | Cholent | Orisa | Sauerbraten | Gedempte fleisch | Msoki

Chicken liver knishes

Knishes (pronounce the 'k' and the 'n') are stuffed pasties, akin to piroshki, traditionally made with potato, kasha, liver or cheese. In the US, where the knish has flourished since its transplantation from Eastern Europe, they come in all shapes, forms and fillings, from one-bite weenies to doorstop substitutes. This recipe, from Cass Chaya Hirsch, an American-Jewish filmmaker based in Berlin, was handed down from her great-grandmother Yente Jershalimsky ("Yes, that was her real name so, of course, she changed it to Yedda!") of Lvov, Poland.

The other side of Cass's family were also keen cooks, as well as active radicals; her grandmother Sheyna, from Horodetz in Poland, always claimed that one famous night Trotsky came to dinner. Cass says, "I've never really believed the legend, but I appreciate the values the story expresses in a family of generations of communists. But I still wonder what they might have served Trotsky? Perhaps my bubbe's famous *prokus* (meatballs stuffed with cabbage) or the honey cake she learned from Esther, her mother. Or maybe something like these potato knishes stuffed with chicken liver?"

In Poland, the recipe was probably made with schmaltz (chicken fat) rather than margarine, but Cass's family recipe originally included the shocking, subversive use of butter. The knish as political statement. *Oy gevalt*, comrades.

MAKES 25–30 KNISHES

PASTRY

9 tbsp firm margarine, cut into small cubes, plus extra for frying

2½ cups all-purpose flour sifted with 2 tsp baking powder and 1 tsp salt

1 egg, mixed with ⅝ cup water

FILLING

4 tbsp margarine

2 onions, finely chopped

1 oz mushrooms, sliced (optional)

anywhere between ½ lb and 1 lb chicken livers

1 lb 2 oz potatoes, boiled in salted water and mashed or passed through a potato ricer

3 eggs, whisked

½ cup all-purpose flour, sifted

1 tsp salt

½ tsp pepper

2 tbsp very finely grated onion

MAKE the pastry by first cutting the margarine into the flour with two knives. Stir in the egg and water until the pastry forms a ball. Chill for an hour while you make the filling.

MELT a little margarine in a frying pan and gently fry the onions until they are soft. Add the mushrooms, and then the chicken livers and sauté for about 10 minutes. Grind briefly in the food processor and set aside to cool.

MELT half the margarine and add to the potatoes along with the eggs, flour, salt, pepper and grated onion. Knead until smooth. Take a small ball of mashed potato, use your finger to make a pocket in the center and fill with some chicken liver mixture. Chill in the fridge until you're ready to assemble the knishes.

PREHEAT the oven to 375°F.

SPRINKLE a clean work surface with flour and knead until smooth.

ROLL the dough as thinly as possible on a lightly floured surface; keep stretching the dough, as it has a tendency to bounce back.

CUT into 3-inch circles. Place a chicken-liver-filled potato ball in a dough circle, fold over and pinch the edges firmly together.

MELT the remaining margarine and use to seal the edges.

BRUSH with the egg and water, place on a greased baking sheet and bake for 20 minutes until brown.

Note: In the kosher Jewish kitchen, liver must be bought either certified kosher or koshered at home in order to remove all blood.

Chopped liver

Some people make chopped liver with chicken livers, others with ox liver or a mix of the two; some go easy on the eggs or include raw onion. For me, it has to be chicken, schmaltz, slow-cooked onions and plenty of boiled eggs. Barmitzvah boy, King Kong and naked lady sculptures are undertaken at your own risk.

As the late, great columnist, Chaim Bermant, once parodied: "Better a meal of herbs and love therewith, than a stalled ox and hate therewith, but better still a plate of chopped liver."

FRY the onion slowly in the schmaltz until soft and light golden brown.
ADD the chicken livers and fry until tender. Set aside to cool.
MINCE, finely chop or briefly grind in a food processor the liver, onion and two of the eggs with salt and pepper. The texture should not be too smooth – this is not chicken liver pâté. Season to taste.
SERVE garnished with the remaining egg, finely chopped.

SERVES 4
1 large onion, chopped
3 tbsp schmaltz – accept no substitutes. Cut down on the schmaltz and it's not Jewish cooking.

8 oz chicken livers
3 hard-boiled eggs
salt and white pepper

"How just is the Lord. He gives food to the rich – and an appetite to the poor." JEWISH SAYING

ABOVE: SABBATH KIDDUSH, KIEV, UKRAINE

Mushroom & barley soup
Krupnik

A comforting, cold-weather soup that can be made with vegetable stock, but really needs the depth of a good chicken or beef broth. In Eastern Europe, home-dried wild mushrooms were part of everyone's pantry and do add that essential whiff of the Urals. Apart from the mushrooms and barley, the basic ingredients are onion, carrot and celery – the holy trinity of Yiddish vegetables, you should pardon the expression.

SERVES 4–6

a few dried cèpe mushrooms, soaked in a little water for 10 minutes, drained (reserve the liquid) and chopped
9 oz fresh mushrooms, chopped
1 large onion, chopped
3–4 carrots, chopped
4 celery sticks, chopped
1½ cups barley
freshly grated nutmeg
salt and pepper
chopped thyme
4⅓ cups chicken or beef stock
4⅓ cups water
chopped dill and parsley

PUT all the ingredients, except the stock, water, dill and parsley, in a big pot (preferably one that your bubbe schlepped all the way from *der heim* on her back), cover with the stock, water and liquid from the dried mushrooms. Bring slowly to a boil, season, then turn the heat down low and simmer gently, covered, for about 2 hours.
SERVE sprinkled with the dill and parsley, and accompanied by rye or black bread.

Lamb & lentil soup with cumin

A recipe from Eran Harel, talented Israeli-born executive chef of the innovative and much praised restaurant at Berlin's Jewish Museum, named after the painter, Max Liebermann, one of the greatest German Impressionists of his day.

The dish is a cross between goulash and a biblical mess of potage, and also a meal in one bowl (which always saves on the washing up).

SERVES 10

7 oz onions, finely chopped
5 oz leeks, finely sliced
¼ cup olive oil
6 garlic cloves, finely chopped
2 lb 4 oz lamb, cut into ¾-inch cubes
¼ cup tomato paste
2 tbsp cumin seeds
6⅞ cups hot lamb stock
2 cups dried red lentils
7 oz tomatoes, chopped
salt and pepper
juice of 1 lemon
7 oz fresh cilantro, finely chopped

SOFTEN the onions and leek in the olive oil until the onion starts to turn golden, then add the garlic.
ADD the lamb in batches and brown on all sides, then stir in the tomato paste and cumin seeds.
ADD the stock and simmer for 30 minutes, stirring occasionally.
ADD the lentils and tomatoes and simmer for another 30 minutes. If necessary, add water.
JUST before serving, adjust the seasonings and stir in the lemon juice and cilantro.

LEFT: MUSHROOM & BARLEY SOUP

Yemenite meat soup
A recipe from Ayala Bleys

Although she now lives in Antwerp, Ayala was born in the Yemenite quarter of Tel Aviv, a network of noisy alleys that run between the Carmel Market and the sea. The Jewish community in Yemen dates back to the destruction of the Second Temple, if not much earlier. In the 4th and 5th centuries, Yemen was even ruled by Jewish monarchs, but after the arrival of Islam in the 8th century their lives became increasingly restricted. Jews were forbidden to leave the country, and the community was isolated for centuries. Ironically, this helped preserve many elements of ancient Hebrew culture that disappeared from other parts of the Jewish world. From the 19th century until the founding of the state of Israel, 16,000 Yemenite Jews emigrated to Palestine, often making the journey on foot. Many others were to come in 1949 with Operation Magic Carpet, an airlift that transferred virtually all the remaining two-thirds of the community to Israel, fulfilling an old prophecy that one day a great bird would take them back to the Holy Land.

Yemenite Jews have always been renowned as artisans, especially for their silverwork and intricate jewelry as delicately wrought as their own fine features. A highly pious community, they have also preserved their own synagogue music and melodies – and their distinctive way of cooking, which probably most resembles the Jewish food of biblical times. This soup is one Ayala remembers her grandmother making; her own daughter now takes pots of it with her back to school. Ayala makes it much as her grandmother did, except she buys the z'hug ready-made instead of laboriously preparing and pounding it by hand. She is a passionate advocate, also, of the health-giving properties of the fenugreek that goes into her beloved hilbe, which accompanies the soup and almost everything else she eats. ("It's good for your heart, blood, cholesterol, digestion... my husband is a doctor and he has really researched this!"). When Ayala visits her mother in Israel, the thing she most craves is "kubbanah (a buttery, moist bread cooked overnight in a special pot for the Sabbath) with hilbe and an egg!"

Yemenite food is simple, she explained, based mostly on soup, breads baked in a clay oven, and a little meat, including organ meats, as well as grains, nuts and spices. In Arabia, locusts were a delicacy, but the ritual of the hunt is now just the subject of old men's reminiscences. On the Sabbath they make special blessings over ga'le, nuts and dried fruit, and have this traditional hot and peppery soup. "It makes a whole meal, but everyone's version is slightly different; the meat cut differently, or a different spice mixture. For example, I cut my vegetables much smaller than many do." Ayala's grandmother had a special basalt curved chopping block and stone, and a pestle and mortar for the fenugreek seeds, "but now everyone has a food mixer!"

On special occasions, the Yemenite table is strewn with vegetables and salad leaves, which look very beautiful in context, but is probably not a good idea otherwise, unless you want your dining room to look like a supermarket's produce section.

Hawayij – a homemade spice blend – can vary, as do those sold in the markets of Jerusalem and Tel Aviv. Ayala, however, uses a store-bought Israeli spice mix, but if you can't find any, she suggests the following: 2 tbsp cumin, 1 tbsp turmeric, 1 tbsp ground black pepper plus 2–3 cloves of finely chopped garlic and salt, to taste. (Ground black caraway seed may also be included.)

SERVES 6

1 lb 2 oz stewing beef
hawayij (see quantity above)
2 potatoes, diced
3 onions, finely chopped
4 carrots, peeled and sliced
2 slices of pumpkin, diced
1 celery stick with the leaves, chopped
bunch of fresh parsley, roughly chopped

PLACE the meat in a large pot and cover with water. Bring to a boil and remove any scum from the surface.
ADD the spices, cover and simmer for about 20 minutes.
ADD the vegetables and parsley, cover and simmer until the meat is tender and the vegetables are soft (about 45 minutes). This is best prepared the day before, chilled and any fat removed that has formed on top of the soup.

The soup is served with z'hug, a highly spiced sauce made of hot green peppers, cilantro and garlic that has become popular throughout Israel, and hilbe, ground fenugreek seeds (a symbol of fertility, especially at the New Year) soaked overnight in salted water, then beaten until thick and creamy and flavored with more z'hug.

Chicken soup

When it comes to symbols, this is the mother icon of the Jewish Kitchen. I promised myself the words "Jewish penicillin" would never cross my lips, except to say its virtues were even recognized by Maimonides, who regarded it as "beneficial for the feeble-bodied" centuries before it was SCIENTIFICALLY proven to cure all ills.

Golden chicken soup, the color of prosperity, unites all parts of the Jewish world, especially on a Friday night, but variations on the theme are simply endless. Everyone has their own trick to put a little *neshome* (soul) into the soup: onion skins, saffron, tomato, garlic, dill, a pinch of sugar or maybe, yes, even a bouillon cube. You could debate ingredients, technique or desired color until *Moshiach* (the Messiah) comes, not to mention the garnishes, of which the following three recipes are but a small selection, but space is short and I know you're all anxious to discover my own, special family ingredient.

SERVES 6–8

For Jewish chicken soup, first you need a Jewish chicken or one large boiling hen with all the necks, gizzards, feet, etc., you can lay your hands on (sad little modern roasters just don't work the same magic). Kosher fowl, salted to remove the blood, also make for clearer broth and better flavor.

small piece of fore shank beef – a bit more or a bit less won't make a lot of difference. This is the secret!
2–3 tsp salt
a few black peppercorns
2½–3 quarts cold water
1 large onion, roughly chopped
1 large carrot, thickly sliced
1 celery stick, chopped
2 bay leaves

WASH the chicken thoroughly. Place in a large pan with the beef and seasonings and cover with the water. Bring slowly to a boil and skim well. Reduce the heat.

ADD the rest of the ingredients, cover the pan and simmer for a good 2 hours. Strain off the liquid, let cool and refrigerate overnight. Reserve the carrots. The following day, skim the fat from the surface of the soup.

REHEAT the soup with the reserved carrots and serve with knaidlach, lokshen, or mandlen (see pages 70–71) or with kreplach (like Jewish ravioli). Inhale deeply and eat while it's still hot.

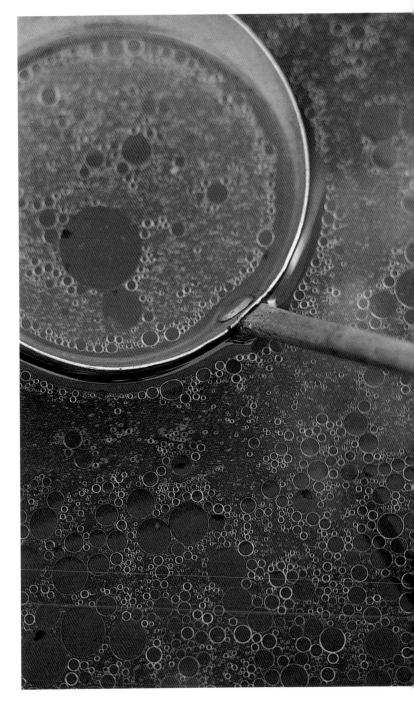

LEFT: NOODLES AND PASTA
(FOR CHICKEN SOUP)

Zena Swerling's knaidlach
Matzo balls

Opinions divide on knaidlach (major understatement). You either like them with or without chicken fat, soft or firm, floaters or sinkers, light as a feather or the cannonballs favored by Golda Meir. These knaidlach from Zena Swerling, one of Manchester, England's, finest cooks, are guaranteed to be light and fluffy every time.

"TO MAKE A LOT"

4 eggs

¾ cup sunflower oil plus a little extra

salt and white pepper, to taste

⅝ cup cold water

medium matzo meal

⅝ cup boiling water

some chicken stock, for cooking

BEAT the eggs, oil, seasoning, and water, then slowly add enough matzo meal to make a thick mixture. Add the boiling water, mix well and let stand for at least an hour.

PUT some oil on a tray and rub your hands with oil as well. Roll the mixture into balls about the size of large whole walnuts.

BRING a large pan of water and some chicken stock to a rapid boil. Drop in the balls, lower the heat and simmer, half-covered, for about 30 minutes.

ALLOW to cool then remove with a draining spoon.

REHEAT separately and add to the soup when serving. "Only reheat the balls in the chicken soup if you want to ruin it."

Mrs. Frazer's soup mandlen

Freda Frazer's soup *mandlen* (nuts) are renowned in Manchester, England. She learned them from her mother, who came to the UK from Russia as a young girl.

"MAKES ENOUGH FOR A LARGE FAMILY"
2 eggs
salt

1¼ cups self-rising flour
vegetable oil, for frying

BEAT the eggs with a pinch of salt.

SPRINKLE the flour on to a board. Make a well and add the eggs. Gradually incorporate the flour into the eggs. If the paste seems too stiff, add a little water.

KNEAD, roll and cut into strips, like pencils. Then "chop, chop, chop" into little triangular shapes.

SHALLOW-FRY in ¾ inch of hot oil, turning so they brown on both sides, or deep-fry for a few minutes in oil heated to 350°F. Drain and serve with chicken soup (see page 69).

Samuels family lokshen

A recipe from another good friend, Ruth Kaitiff, who came to the UK with her Ukrainian grandmother and makes a delicious – and filling – alternative to standard soup noodles. But, as they used to say in *der alter welt* when they measured health and beauty by bulk, you should be *gezunt und shtark* (healthy and fat). Ah, those were the days.

SERVES 6–8
7 oz box of broad lokshen (egg noodles) ("It's got to be broad, it doesn't work with fine lokshen.")

2 eggs, beaten
salt and pepper
2 tbsp margarine or schmaltz

PREHEAT the oven to 350°F.

COOK the lokshen according to the package instructions, drain and set aside to cool.

MIX the lokshen with the eggs and seasoning. Set aside.

PUT the fat in a 1 quart ovenproof bowl and place in the oven until the fat melts and starts to spit. CAREFULLY remove from the oven and swirl the hot fat around the side of the bowl.

ADD the lokshen mixture to the bowl and put back into the oven. Turn the heat up a little and bake for about 50 minutes, or until the lokshen is golden brown and looks very crispy.

PUT a slice in each soup bowl before ladling over the chicken soup.

"Love is grand, but love with lokshen is even better." YIDDISH PROVERB

71

On the tradewinds of freedom

WE SANG THE HAUNTING MELODY OF THE ANCIENT SEPHARDI PRAYER
"BENDIGAMOS Á EL ALTÍSIMO" AFTER FRIDAY NIGHT DINNER AT THE HOME OF
RUTH AND CHARLES GOMEZ CASSERES IN CURAÇAO, IN THE DUTCH ANTILLES.

As we ate *sòpi di galiña*, Charles recounted how both belonged to Spanish-Portuguese families who were among the first to find refuge from the Inquisition "on the tradewinds of freedom." Their ancestors were founders of the island's exquisite Mikvé Israel-Emanuel synagogue or *snoa*, the oldest in the New World to remain in continuous use since its consecration in 1732.

Curaçao is a postage stamp of an island; a half-forgotten name from the tissue pages of a childhood album. Yet it has been a haven for over 40 different races and religions, a microcosm of tolerance floating off the great land mass of South America. The synagogue stands in the center of Willemstad, the island's main (and only) town, and a beguiling stewpot of Caribbean rhythms, Latin style, Dutch order and European sensibilities. The gabled roofs and formal lines of the restored Colonial houses are softened by carnival shades of aqua and apricot, banana and green. Two streets away, the daily market is augmented by a flotilla of fish, spice and vegetable sellers from Venezuela. The town, which is on the World Heritage List, is divided by the world's largest pedestrian pontoon bridge, swinging open throughout the day to allow ships and tankers into the immense natural harbor that was always a magnet for European empire-builders.

The very first Jew to set foot on the tiny island was Samuel Coheno in 1634, an interpreter for the Dutch fleet that won the island from the Spanish. Over the next 30 years, he was followed by other colonists, who brought with them from Amsterdam a *Sefer Torah* (scroll of the Law), and the blessings of their families.

When I asked Charles how these early pioneers, in their quest for religious freedom and safety, kept their faith in the face of savage seas, scorched, barren soil and back-breaking toil, he explained, "Today, it is easy to be an unaffiliated Jew, but in those days if you were not a member of a congregation you were out of things, everyone belonged to some sort of church."

Although some went into agriculture – Curaçao liqueur, based on orange peel, is derived from the failure of naranja orange trees to thrive – most became somewhat unlikely seafarers, ship-builders and shipping merchants. To boost their courage against storms and pirates, they gave their ships Hebrew names, sailing forth with prayer shawls and phylacteries. The risks were enormous but, throughout, the colonists kept in constant touch with their community elders in Amsterdam, arguing points of religious law with a fervor undiminished by distance.

In the 18th century, Curaçao became known as the "Mother Community of the Americas," helping to establish synagogues elsewhere in the New World. Thanks, in part, to the international connections and language skills of its Jewish citizens, Curaçao had become a prosperous commercial crossroads. Jewish companies were granted permission to mint their own coins and issue their own

"Behind the high golden walls, it is a place out of time. A true sanctuary for centuries…"

CLOCKWISE FROM TOP CENTER:
FLOATING MARKET, CURAÇAO;
SYNAGOGUE ENTRANCE;
SYNAGOGUE MUSEUM;
SHOP IN WILLEMSTAD, CURAÇAO;
WATERFRONT SNACK BAR

stamps. They built fine buildings and Italianate mansions, quays and wharves; culturally, as Charles, community historian, has written, "they produced scores of doctors, several noted jurists, many civil servants, newspaper and periodical publishers, poets and authors." As well as the distinguished World War II hero George Maduro.

The beautiful synagogue is a testament to their sense of Jewish continuity. Behind the high golden walls, it is a place out of time. A true sanctuary for centuries: cobalt-blue glass windows, lofty stone pillars, dark mahogany hand-carved from Haitian wood against whitewashed walls. On special occasions, the interior glows from the shimmering candles on the immense Dutch brass chandeliers. The imposing 18th-century pipe organ is the only one of its kind outside the Netherlands. At its peak, in the 1780s, the congregation numbered 2,000, and the synagogue reflects their pride, prosperity and devotion.

On the floor there is a thick carpet of white sand, laid down both in remembrance of the Exodus, and the precautions taken to muffle the sound of footsteps when Jews had to worship secretly during the Inquisition; some of the service is still conducted in Portuguese. In the small museum, there is an ancient *mikva* (religious bath), a *Sefer Torah* dating from medieval Spain, 300-year old circumcision chairs, and an 18th-century silver tray that is still used for the glass-breaking ceremony at weddings. A 1901 greeting card is inscribed from the Good Luck Sunday Morning Walking and Coffee Drinking Club.

It is easy to imagine the ladies of Curaçao enjoying their refreshments in much the same manner as I was so generously received over a century later. Technology may have changed, but they still partake of *banket* (almond cookies), hot milk cake, *bolo di manteka* (butter cake), *sunchi* (meringue kisses) and, for every special occasion, *panlevi* (crisp sponge cookies).

All these recipes are in a book, *Recipes from the Jewish Kitchens of Curaçao*, compiled by the synagogue sisterhood. Many recipes, as Ruth Gomes Casseres explained, are unique to the island, and reflect a colorful mix of cultures and influences. From the Afro-Caribbean tradition come recipes for plantains, *kala* (black-eyed pea puffs), okra soup, curried peanut chicken and *funchi* (cornmeal mush). Edam or Gouda cheese go into *tekeno* (cheese sticks in pastry), and Dutch heritage is also evident in *appeltaart* and Indonesian saté. The trading links with British colonies have left an intriguing taste for ketchup, piccalilli and Worcestershire sauce.

But the majority of recipes derive from their own Sephardi roots: arroz con pollo; pickled fish; borekas; sweet and sour tongue with capers, olives, raisins and prunes. The festivals are the time for special traditions. To break the Yom Kippur fast, warm sangria, spiced with cinnamon, nutmeg and green limes is served with heated rolls. At the end of the meal, coffee is topped with *webu bati*, a blend of eggs, sugar and vanilla. At Passover, an unusual charoset packed with fruit and nuts is shaped into balls and rolled in cinnamon. For wedding parties, there is the magnificent *bolo pretu* or bride's cake, a superb, liqueur-packed creation that takes weeks of preparation.

The oldest surviving Jewish congregation in the New World. The oldest synagogue in uninterrupted use in the Western Hemisphere. The oldest Jewish burial ground in the Americas. The Spanish-Portuguese Jews of Curaçao have much of which they can be proud, and possess a very real love for their pride and joy, their *snoa*.

The synagogue is filled with light and warmth. It is appropriate. Light is the symbol of the Divine; the Divine symbolizes hope… the hope of Israel – Mikvé Israel. Each and every Sabbath, the congregants leave their footprints in the sand. As they say, "A people without a past has no future."

Curaçao chicken soup
Sòpi di galiña

SERVES 4–6

1 chicken (about 2 lb 12 oz)

2–3 fresh limes

3 celery stalks, diced

2 green peppers, chopped

1 small onion, sliced

1 garlic clove, finely chopped

3 carrots, thickly sliced

2 scallions, chopped

2 tomatoes, chopped

2 tbsp tomato paste

1 lb soup bones

3 bouillon cubes

1 sweet corn

4–5 potatoes, cut into chunks

about 3½ oz vermicelli
   (or more, if preferred)

Worcestershire sauce (optional)

WASH the chicken and rub all over with lime juice. Put into a large soup pot with the vegetables (except the potatoes and sweet corn), tomato paste and the bones. Add enough water to cover the chicken, vegetables and bones. Bring to a boil and skim off any foam. Reduce the heat and simmer, covered, for about 45 minutes.

STRAIN the stock and add the bouillon cubes. Discard the soup bones and all the vegetables except the carrots. Skin and bone the chicken and cut into bite-size pieces.

BOIL the sweet corn until tender, cool and cut into chunks.

COOK the potatoes in the chicken broth, and when nearly done add the vermicelli. Stir in the chicken, carrots and sweet corn. If desired, add a dash of Worcestershire sauce to spice the soup.

"Zjanta ku zjeitu!" OLD PAPIAMENTU FOR "ENJOY!"

Bukharan plov

Two versions of this famous Bukharan Friday night and festival dish. Similar ingredients, but different techniques and even different names make for contrasting dishes.

This first recipe for *plov* comes from Liz and Lawrence Yusupoff of Manchester, England. Lawrence's grandparents originated variously from Bukhara, Tashkent, Samarkand and Kabul. The Bukharan Jewish community is said to date back 2,500 years, and were involved in the silk trade for centuries as merchants and dyers. Lawrence still possesses some of the exquisite embroidered silk ceremonial robes and prayer caps his family brought with them when they emigrated.

Bukharan cooking is influenced by its location as one of the original crossroads of the world; from China come noodle soups, from India, savory samosas, from Tibet, steamed dumplings and from Persia, kebabs. But they are perhaps most famed for their wonderful rice dishes. Liz was instructed in the preparation of this dish by her mother-in-law, Giselle, although she has since added her own variation. Giselle, who was brought up in Paris, also presented her with a special *râpeur* with which to grate the carrots to the requisite length. Lawrence, however, still doubts whether they are sufficiently long and fine, but as Liz says, "That's typical of Bukharan men. They like to do the food shopping but won't cook themselves, although they're always very happy to pass comment...." Hmmmm. Liz also adds that the plov must be eaten with the salad for proper balance.

SERVES 6

2¼ cups long-grain rice, covered with boiling water and left to soak while the other ingredients are prepared

1 cup plus 1 tbsp raisins, also set aside to soak in boiling water

SALAD

½ cucumber, finely diced

1 shallot or scallion, finely chopped

2 tomatoes, finely chopped

2 large onions, finely chopped

3–4 tbsp vegetable oil

1 large chicken, cut into 8 pieces (with the skin ON! – a must for flavor)

1 lb 10 oz carrots, grated into long julienne strips

salt and freshly ground black pepper

juice of ½ lemon

½ tsp sugar

masses of finely chopped cilantro

salt and pepper

FRY the onions with a little of the carrot in the oil in a large stovetop casserole dish. Add salt and plenty of pepper (about 12 grinds).

ADD the chicken, a bit more salt and another 10 grinds of pepper. Stir it around a bit, then cover and leave for a good 30 minutes on a low heat.

COVER with the remaining carrots and more salt and black pepper. The chicken should be gently bubbling away by now. Drain the raisins and sprinkle them over the carrots.

SCOOP up the rice with a slotted spoon (don't drain it completely, it needs to be slightly sloppy) and arrange over the carrots and raisins. Cover and cook over a low heat for another 1¼ hours until a fragrant, toasty aroma emerges from the pot.

MAKE the salad by combining all the ingredients.

LEFT: JEWISH SHOEMAKERS,
BUKHARA, UZBEKISTAN

Bukharan carrot pilav

Rachel Soleyman now lives in Antwerp, Netherlands, but was born in
Kabul, Afghanistan, and raised in Bombay. She has lived in many parts
of the world, but this recipe has always traveled with her.

SERVES 8

3¼ cups Basmati rice

2 tbsp plus 1 tsp salt

1 large onion, finely chopped

6 tbsp vegetable oil

2 lb 4 oz beef, veal or lamb, cut
   into large cubes

1 medium chicken, cut into
   8 pieces

3 lb 5 oz carrots, cut into long
   julienne strips

½ tsp freshly ground black
   pepper

2 tsp sugar

2½ tbsp ground cinnamon

⅞ cup golden raisins

BOIL the rice with the 2 tablespoons of salt until three-quarters
cooked. Drain and set aside.

FRY the onion in half the oil in a large, stovetop casserole dish, add the
meat, cover and cook for 30 minutes.

ADD the chicken, a small handful of the carrots, and the pepper, then
replace the lid and cook for another 30 minutes.

POUR about half a cup of gravy from the casserole dish into another
large pot. Add half of the remaining carrots and sprinkle with 1
teaspoon of the sugar, ½ teaspoon of the salt and 1 tablespoon of the
cinnamon. Repeat the layering.

POUR the chicken and meat from the other casserole dish over the
carrots and add the remaining cinnamon. Cover and cook over a low
heat until the carrots are tender, then add the golden raisins.

TOP with the almost-cooked rice. Lay a clean dish towel across the pot,
and cover with the lid. Steam for about 15 minutes.

Georgian chicken
Chakhokhbili

When it comes to sheer vitality and enjoyment at the table, Georgian Jews have few equals, with their immense capacity for legendary feasts and banquets, music and dance. Jews have lived in the ancient kingdom of Georgia for well over 2,500 years, managing to sustain their communal religious life even throughout the years of Soviet repression. Although many have now emigrated to Israel or the US, they remain fiercely proud of their cooking, which draws on the region's wealth of fresh fruit, vegetables, cheese, honey, grapes and herbs. Indeed, an old Georgian legend tells how God tripped over the Caucasus and scattered the content of his plate on to the land below. Sauces and relishes are made from walnuts, sour plums and pomegranates, and favorite dishes include grilled meats, stuffed breads, walnut dumplings and this richly flavored stew.

SERVES 4

1 medium chicken, divided into 8 pieces

2 tbsp oil

2 large onions, finely chopped

1 lb potatoes, peeled and parboiled

1¾ cup thick tomato sauce

1 tsp turmeric or a few saffron threads dissolved in a little hot water

1 tsp each ground coriander, hot paprika, fenugreek and salt

2 bay leaves

⅞ cup red wine

2 tbsp fresh herbs, chopped – use singly or any combination of cilantro, parsley, basil or mint

PUT the chicken into a large sauté pan with the oil. Cook, covered, over a low heat for 5 minutes, then remove the lid and cook for another 10 minutes turning the chicken over once or twice to brown both sides.

ADD the onion and cook for another 10 minutes, stirring the chicken around so the onions soften.

ADD the potatoes, tomato sauce, spices, bay leaves and wine. Stir well so the chicken is coated in the sauce. Bring to a boil, then cover and turn the heat down to a simmer. Cook for about 20–30 minutes more until the chicken is tender and the sauce quite thick. Give it a stir from time to time to make sure nothing sticks.

TAKE off the heat, season with the herbs, put the lid back on and allow to stand for 5 minutes before serving.

Moroccan chicken with dates

"The righteous shall flourish like the palm tree." – Psalm 92:13
Bunches of dark, ripe dates, provocatively veiled in dark net, dangle
from mop-head palms stretching up into the azure sky. A squadron
of pelicans flies in low formation over the river Jordan en route to
winter camp.

The trees were planted by the descendants of urban German
Jews, who brought with them a mix of religious ideals and democratic
socialism. They also brought an unusual interest in age-old methods
of farming, plus a pioneering concern for environmental issues.
Today, Kibbutz Sde Eliyahu is one of Israel's leading organic farms,
and their 175 acres of old Templar land is worked on eco-friendly,
integrated principles. It is an Old Testament approach to the food
chain – and a sticky mouthful of Bible history. Scholars believe the
honey referred to in the phrase "milk and honey" refers to the
concentrated juice of the date, one of the world's oldest cultivated
fruits. The fruit plays an important role in Jewish tradition, especially
at the New Year, when it is considered a symbol of sweetness. The
Hebrew word for date also sounds like part of the blessing in which
we ask for our sins to be forgiven.

This recipe comes from Gaby Nonhoff of Berlin, who enjoyed it
many years ago at the home of her Moroccan neighbor in Israel.
Claudia Roden suggests this combination of flavors has roots that
go back to medieval Baghdad.

SERVES 6

1¾ cups Mejdool dates, pitted
juice of 1 lemon
3 large onions, finely chopped
2 tbsp vegetable oil
2 cups lightly toasted whole,
  blanched almonds
1½ tsp cinnamon mixed with
  ½ tsp mace, ¼ tsp nutmeg,
  ½ tsp white pepper and salt
1 large chicken, cleaned and
  salted inside and out

1 tsp powdered saffron
  (or a few threads soaked in
  warm water)
1 tbsp honey
2 tbsp water
1 cup plus 2 tbsp toasted sliced
  almonds, to garnish

STEEP the dates in the lemon juice for 1 hour.

FRY the onions slowly in the oil until transparent. Let cool.

STUFF each date with an almond and some onion, and roll in the
spice mix.

STUFF the chicken with the dates. Sew up or skewer the cavity
opening. Use any leftover dates to surround the chicken when it
goes into the pot.

ADD the saffron to the remaining spice mixture and rub the outside of
the chicken with it.

COVER the bottom of a stovetop casserole dish with the remaining
onions and add the chicken. Drizzle over the honey and water, cover
and stew gently for 1¾–2 hours until very tender. Baste occasionally,
adding a little more water if necessary.

CAREFULLY remove the chicken to a large platter, and open up the
cavity so you can spoon out the stuffing. Garnish with some of the
sauce and with the toasted almonds.

SERVE with saffron rice and salad.

Green masala chicken curry

The ancient Bene Israel community, the largest of the three groups of Jews in India, are believed to have arrived in India after they fled the cruel reign of Antiochus Epiphanes in Judea. According to oral tradition, they were shipwrecked on the sea journey and lost their only copy of the Torah; working as farmers, soldiers and pressers of oil, these "Children of Israel" somehow sustained their religious identity throughout the centuries of separation from mainstream Jewry until they returned to the fold, like lost lambs, after 2,000 years.

This recipe was kindly given me by Mrs. Rivka Elias of Bombay who says it is always prepared during the High Holidays and for weddings and parties. Passed down from generation to generation, every home has its own version. When I asked Rivka if she had a story about the recipe, this was her reply:

"A story about this recipe? Well, when my sons were at home in India, they always grumbled about eating curries. In fact, Ari actually told my friend Eva, 'I'm so bored with the food at home.' Eva said, 'But I always enjoy your mother's cooking: She makes green curry, red curry, brown curry.' And Ari replied, 'Yes, but they all taste the same to me!' Now when I go to the USA, I always have to make my green curry for my sons and all their friends. How their taste has changed."

Also popular at the New Year and Yom Kippur, when the entire congregation dresses in white, is a colorful halva made with coconut milk and sprinkled with pistachios that takes hours of constant stirring. It is usually made in large quantities "because every family takes several platefuls to distribute to other Jewish families after prayers."

SERVES 4
3 tbsp oil (any sort)
1 large onion, finely chopped
1 large tomato, finely chopped
1 lb skinless, boneless chicken
salt, to taste
14 fl oz can unsweetened coconut milk

MASALA
1 oz cilantro leaves
1-inch piece fresh ginger, grated
5 garlic cloves
6–8 small green chilies (seeded, if preferred)
1 tsp fennel seeds
1-inch cinnamon stick
seeds from 1 cardamom pod
2 cloves
8 black peppercorns
½ tsp turmeric

FRY the onions in the oil in a large pot until golden brown. Add the tomato and cook until any liquid evaporates and the onion and tomato become paste-like.

MAKE the masala by grinding or pounding all the ingredients together to make a green paste.

ADD the masala to the pot and cook until the color changes from bright to deep green and the oil starts to separate. "When you get the aroma of the masala, then you know it's cooked."

ADD the chicken and salt, and cook at medium heat for 20 minutes. Once the chicken is cooked, add the coconut milk and remove from heat after 1 minute. Eat with steamed white rice.

The curry can be reheated, but do so carefully otherwise the coconut milk may curdle.

Persian jeweled rice with chicken

The Persian Jewish community is one of the oldest in the Diaspora, dating back 90 generations to the destruction of the First Temple and the time of Cyrus the Great. Their history, however, has been one of persecution, discrimination and enforced conversion interspersed with brief periods of tolerance. The greatest period of prosperity was under the Phalevi dynasty, but the 1979 revolution forced around half of the 100,000 strong community to flee the country, mostly to the US and Israel. Although officially recognized as a minority group, life for those remaining (estimates vary between 12,000 and 25,000) is precarious, especially following the 1999 show trials of 13 Jews in Shiraz on spying charges.

The close-knit exiles have brought with them a love of Persian language and culture, as well as a wonderful range of gently spiced dishes, a remarkable skill with cooking rice, and specialities such as this festive New Year chicken.

SERVES 6

2⅛ cups Basmati rice

3 lb 5 oz roaster chicken

2 large onions, chopped

salt

rind of 1 large orange (without any pith), finely shredded

2 large carrots, cut into fine slivers

1 cup sugar

4 tbsp sunflower oil

1 cup raisins

1 cup dried barberries or cherries

1 cup dried apricots

a few saffron threads, dissolved in 2 tbsp hot water (optional)

slivered almonds and chopped pistachios, to garnish

RINSE the rice well and let it soak in cold, salted water for several hours.

PLACE the chicken, one of the chopped onions and a little salt in a nonstick pan. Cover and cook over a very low heat – without water – for about 45 minutes. The chicken will simmer in its own fat and juices. Cool, then bone and skin the chicken and cut into small pieces. Set aside, reserving any chicken juices for later use.

PLACE the orange rind, carrots and sugar in a saucepan and cover with 1¼ cups water. Boil for 10 minutes, then drain.

FRY the other onion gently in 2 tablespoons oil in a frying pan. When translucent add the raisins, barberries and apricots and cook for another few minutes. Add the orange and carrot mixture, then set aside. Drain, reserving any oil.

IN a large nonstick or heavy-bottomed saucepan, bring 1½ quarts water to a boil with 1 tablespoon salt. Drain the rice and add to the pan. Bring back to a boil and immediately lower the heat so the rice simmers gently for about 3 minutes until it is parboiled. Drain, rinse with tepid water, shake gently in a sieve to keep the grains separate and set aside.

WASH out the pan and add the rest of the oil, swirling it around so it covers some of the sides as well as the bottom of the pan.

WITH your hands, sprinkle in a layer of rice (this helps to aerate it). Top with some chicken, then some fruit. Continue, trying to build a conical shape and finishing with a layer of rice. If a pyramid simply won't hold, poke a few holes through the rice with the end of a wooden spoon.

DRIZZLE over the reserved chicken juices, the remaining oil and the saffron. Cover the pan with a clean dish towel, then a tight lid and cook for only 1–2 minutes, over a high heat. Reduce the heat to very low and continue to "steam" for another 40 minutes.

REMOVE from the heat and let stand for 5 minutes before lifting off the lid. Serve in a mound on a large platter, garnished with almonds and pistachios.

(You may need to stand the pan on a cold, wet surface for a minute or two to help remove the crusty bottom layer of rice – the best bit, reserved for honored guests and favorite grandchildren.)

Cubans, "Jewbans"

TO BE A STRANGER IN A STRANGE LAND IS A FAMILIAR JEWISH EXPERIENCE, BUT
THE CUBAN JEWS OF MIAMI COULD NOT HAVE WASHED UP ON A STRANGER SHORE.

Temple Beth Shmuel, home of the Cuban-Hebrew congregation, is located a few blocks, yet another world away, from the never-never, day-glo land by the sea that is South Beach, Florida.

South Beach – so crazy, so weird under the broiling sun, it could only have been invented by madmen and millionaires. The beautiful Art Deco buildings have been restored in dazzling candy shop colors; Ocean Drive is a cavalcade of bronzed triceps, in-line skates, wannabees, porn stars, hucksters, shysters, swaying señoritas and Versace pilgrims, all shimmering to an insistent Latino beat. Even the dogs have attitude. South Beach parades its vanities as other cities offer their culture and commerce. The daily prayer is to accessorize, accessorize, accessorize.

South Beach is a tabloid morality tale where decrepit dowagers sport diamond knuckledusters and slippers made from tire treads; spaced-out junkies speak in tongues; small, tattooed men walk down Lincoln with big, spotted dogs. There is a raffish side to Miami that grows like tumbleweed in the cracks of the palaces to style and hedonism that line the most expensive sandbar in the world. Yet it is here, in the capital of kitsch, that the twice-exiled Cuban-Hebrew congregation has found its refuge, a place where the past can be remembered in peace, and the dead with dignity and respect.

Back in Cuba the community comprised several strands. The first to arrive were a small group of "American" Jews whose origins dated back to the Spanish-American War of 1898. Then came Sephardi Jews from Turkey, Syria and North Africa, and finally, in 1920, Eastern European Jews began to arrive.

For the Ashkenazi immigrants, as former president and administrator of the Temple, Aron Kelton, explained, their sojourn in the safe haven of Cuba was seen initially as a stepping stone to the "golden land" of the US. A xenophobic shift in US policies, however, changed their plans and by the 1930s, Jews were permitted to become Cuban citizens.

Aron's story is a typical one: "My parents arrived from Lithuania and Romania when both were very young. They met and married in Havana, where my father worked as a barber. My grandparents were later killed in the Holocaust and I would always wonder why my parents left them. But after I became a father and grandfather myself, I realized it was the ultimate sacrifice for parents to send their children away, even realizing they were unlikely to see them again." It was a story that was to have an uncanny resonance nearly 40 years later.

Jewish life blossomed in Cuba, like flowers under the tropical sun; the growing community formed a new entrepreneurial class, especially in shoes, clothing and fabric production. They built synagogues and schools, opened cultural centers and started welfare and Zionist organizations.

Slow-talking with a dry sense of humor, Aron recalled life in Havana: "We spoke Spanish in the street, but Yiddish at home, and we ate a typical Eastern European menu, even in the heat. My

South Beach – so crazy, so weird under the broiling sun, it could only have been invented by madmen and millionaires.

CLOCKWISE FROM TOP CENTER:
TEMPLE BETH SHMUEL;
MIAMI FLAMINGO; OCEAN DRIVE
HOTELS; SOUTH BEACH; KOSHER
DINING IN FLORIDA

LEFT: HAVANA, CUBA

mother would buy flanken, usually the cheapest cut, from a kosher butcher. One thing we had in common with the Cubans was that we had soup every day. That was our basic meal, chicken or bean soup, but we also had matzo balls, *kishke* and *helzel*!

"Kosher bakers made honey cake, macaroons, rye bread and challah. Gefilte fish, however, had to be made from snapper and grouper. I remember also a famous kosher restaurant in Havana called 'Moishe Pupik,'* but the best kitchen in town was La Co-Operativa, which served wonderful cholent." Prices, too, were a consideration; in Miami's Jewish Museum, an ad from Havana's Fifth Avenue Restaurant boasted "Rates Always Reasonably Moderate."

After Castro came to power in 1959, about 10,000 out of the island's 12,000 Jews fled, mostly to Miami, in the belief they would be back once Cuba returned to normal. It was, however, to become a double diaspora. For the second time in the same century, sometimes in one lifetime, it meant starting over again.

The Cuban-Hebrew congregation was founded in 1961, and as well as a place to pray and gather, it became a conduit that allowed them to transplant themselves into the American-Jewish community without losing their traditions. A *Sefer Torah* brought out of Havana in 1980, symbolically cut the cord that bound them to Cuba, a bittersweet moment.

The "Jewbans" also brought with them an addiction to café Cubano – intense, tiny cups of syrupy-sweet coffee, so strong "it can lift a dead man." They also acquired a new emotional link to dishes such as picadillo and *papas rellenas* (see opposite), *ropa vieja* (beef hash), *arroz con pollo*, black beans and rice, chicken croquettes, meat empanadas, *bistec de palomilla* (steak marinated in garlic and sour orange juice), and exotic fruit and vegetables, especially plantains – sliced, whole, diced, stuffed or made into irresistible crisps called *mariquitas*. Their Cuban desserts include famous ones such as *tres leche*, *churros* and *flan*, as well as guava pastries, the now essential accompaniment to any kiddush.

At weddings and bar mitzvas in the beautiful Olemberg Ballroom ("a five-hour food frenzy!"), where glatt-kosher Cuban food is served beside the sushi and pasta stations, Jewbans sing three anthems: Israeli, American and Free Cuban.

Although memories of life in Cuba – the starry nights, special sunlight and friendly people – have become more distant, they have not faded. Aron was just 30 when he left Cuba with his wife and small child. He worked in a government department and was liable to be arrested at any moment. "My parents didn't want to go, they had been through too much themselves, but they realized I was in danger, so insisted I left. I hate Castro – because of him I could not be with my mother when she died and have never visited her grave. My poor father suffered terribly, and died six months after coming to the States. Life plays so many tricks with you, but the memories are always there.

"Cuba, nonetheless, was a country that welcomed my parents and allowed them to make a living, even though they did not know the language or local customs. We were never rich, simply working people, but we were happy there and I am grateful for that. I have the same feeling about the United States."

As we talked, the redoubtable Mrs. Berta Wodnicki, another Temple stalwart, arrived to pass on a recipe for picadillo: "I know when my husband doesn't like something, because he says he's not hungry and doesn't finish it," she announced, "but, luckily, he likes pretty well everything I make! Anyhow, I can't stay and chat, I have to go home and cook for my son – he's coming by tomorrow and I have to make all his favorite food. You know – *ropa vieja*, picadillo, chicken soup, chicken with plums...." Chicken with plums? "It's an old Russian dish, very good. I was born in Cuba but my family were from Russia." Another story, another dish that has crossed continents. But no time to talk; when a Cuban-Jewish mother needs to feed her son, you don't argue.

*Moishe Pupik: Yiddish speakers will fall down laughing at a restaurant called Moishe Bellybutton – or something more ribald.

Cuban picadillo

With thanks to Berta Wodniki and Ofelia Ruder. Always served with rice, black beans and fried plantains, this is, in Berta's words, "Beautiful, a whole meal."

SERVES 4–6

1 onion, chopped
1–2 tbsp olive oil
1 green pepper, chopped
3 garlic cloves, crushed
1 lb 2 oz ground beef
2 large potatoes, diced (optional)
1 tsp ground cumin (optional)
1 tsp oregano (optional)
1–2 bay leaves
½ cup dry white wine

½ cup tomato paste concentrate
⅓ cup raisins
2 oz pimento-stuffed green olives, chopped
1 tbsp capers
salt and pepper
pinch of sugar
2 tbsp white wine vinegar
chopped parsley and strips of pimento, to garnish (optional)

SAUTÉ the onion in the olive oil until translucent. Add the green pepper and cook until it starts to soften. Add the garlic and, when the aroma rises from the pan, add the beef (and potato, if using).

USE a wooden fork or spoon to make sure the beef browns well without lumps (everyone was most insistent – no lumps. OK?). Stir in the cumin, oregano and bay leaves.

DRAIN OFF any excess fat, then add the wine. Allow to bubble for a few minutes then add the tomato paste concentrate, raisins, olives and capers. Season with salt, pepper and the sugar. Let cook gently for about 30 minutes.

JUST before serving, check the seasoning and add the vinegar.

GARNISH with chopped parsley and strips of pimento, if you like.

VARIATIONS

Venezuelan picadillo

I was given a Venezuelan version of this recipe by Elena Eder of Miami, who says it is the one regularly made in Caracas.

1½ lb ground beef
½ cup water
vegetable oil, for frying
3 tomatoes quartered or 14 oz can with juices

1 green pepper, chopped
3–4 parsley sprigs
1 garlic clove
½ cup wine (any kind)
salt or a bouillon cube

PLACE the beef in a pan, cover with water, bring to a boil, strain and discard the water.

HEAT a little oil in a frying pan, then add the beef. Sauté until brown, add the measured water and cook until absorbed.

PROCESS the remaining ingredients in a blender and add to the beef. Bring to a boil, cover and cook for 30 minutes until the sauce thickens. If needed, season with salt or a bouillon cube. Serve with rice.

Papas rellenas

Leftover picadillo can be used for papas rellenas: dry-mash and season boiled potatoes and allow them to cool. Take a spoonful in the cupped palm of your hand, make a well with a spoon and fill with picadillo. Cover with more mashed potato and shape into balls until the meat is fully enclosed. Dip the rounds in breadcrumbs, beaten egg, then more breadcrumbs. Refrigerate for 1 hour, then fry in 2–3 inches of oil until golden. As Ofelia, mainstay of the Temple Beth Shmuel, says, "Don't make them too big, or too small; but make them all the same, so they line up in the pan like little soldiers."

Holishkes
Stuffed cabbages the Romanian way

This recipe comes from Cynthia Michael, another great Mancunian cook. Although good to eat throughout the year, it is particularly traditional at Sukkot, when stuffed foods symbolize abundance.

Food maven for *The Forward* newspaper in New York, Matthew Goodman has written that just as the Eskimos are said to have numerous words for snow, so do the Jews of Eastern Europe for stuffed cabbage: *holoptshes*, *holishkes* and *geluptzes*, for example, although in the Ukraine the dish was generally known as *prakkes*, a name derived from the Turkish word *yaprak*, or "leaf."

SERVES 8

1½ lb ground beef or lamb

⅞ cup long-grain rice

2 onions, finely chopped

salt and pepper

2 Savoy, green or Dutch white cabbages

vegetable oil, for frying

stock or water, for cooking

2–4 lemons

⅝ cup brown sugar

PREHEAT the oven to 325°F.

MIX the meat, rice, half the onion, salt and pepper and set aside. To remove the cabbage leaves, use a sharp knife to cut a deep cone into the core at the stem end of each cabbage. Plunge the whole cabbages into a large pan of boiling, salted water for 2–3 minutes (this will help loosen the leaves). You may have to do this in batches.

DETACH the leaves from the cabbage and drain them well. Cut out the thick rib from the center of each leaf.

LAY each leaf on a board or plate, place a spoonful of meat in the center and roll up, tucking in both sides to wrap like a small package.

BROWN the rest of the onion in a little oil in a stovetop casserole dish and add the cabbage *holishkes*. Cover with any remaining cabbage leaves.

ADD enough stock or water to cover the cabbage and add some extra seasoning. Cover with a tight fitting lid and bake for at least 3 hours.

NOW add the juice of 2 lemons and about ½ cup brown sugar. Return the casserole dish to the oven for another hour ("The longer the holishkes cook, the better they taste."), then taste to adjust the seasoning, adding more lemon juice and sugar if needed.

Stuffed vegetables from Salonika

This recipe comes from Betty Perahia and uses two techniques typical of Salonikan Jewish cooking: *batuta*, a fried vegetable base, and frying the whole stuffed vegetables. Typically, there is neither onion, garlic nor spices – just good ingredients, with nothing disguised.

SERVES 6–8

peppers, tomatoes, eggplants
  (about a dozen in all)
olive oil, for cooking
2 lb 4 oz ground beef
2 eggs

salt and pepper
breadcrumbs or medium matzo
  meal
1 can chopped tomatoes or
  about 6 fresh tomatoes,
  skinned, seeded and chopped

CUT "lids" off the peppers and carefully remove the seeds. Dice the caps and reserve.

CUT "lids" off the tomatoes, remove the pulp from the interior and set aside. If desired, sprinkle the tomato insides with a little sugar. Dice the caps and add to the pulp.

HALVE the eggplants lengthways and scoop out the inner seeds. Set both aside.

COVER the bottom of a large pan with olive oil. Add the diced pepper, tomato pulp and inner part of the eggplant and let soften over a medium heat. This will make the base of the sauce.

MIX the beef with one of the eggs, season well and stuff the vegetables. If there's any filling left over, use to make small meatballs to cook alongside the stuffed vegetables.

LIGHTLY beat the remaining egg in a shallow dish with a little water. Shake some breadcrumbs or matzo meal into another dish.

DIP the exposed meat surface of each stuffed vegetable into the egg, then into the crumbs.

HEAT a large frying pan with some oil then fry each vegetable, cut side down, to seal the meat. Carefully turn each vegetable to brown lightly on all sides.

ARRANGE the eggplants over the softened vegetables, then make another layer with the tomatoes and peppers. Pour off any residue left in the frying pan.

POUR the canned tomatoes over the stuffed vegetables, cover and simmer for about 30 minutes. To reduce the liquid, remove the lid. In Thessaloníki, this is served at room temperature. In fact, it's a dish that mellows the longer it stands, so can be made the previous day and reheated, as required.

Stuffed onions

The Sinyors have an illustrious pedigree – the last rabbi of Spain was a Sinyor and a Sinyor set sail with Columbus. Other branches of the family, after the Expulsion from Spain and Portugal, went to Italy, Greece, Turkey and then on to Egypt.

Claire Mizrahi was born in the UK to Egyptian-Lebanese parents. She was always passionate about cooking, and after she married Cairo-born Samy Sinyor, learned a number of dishes from his family. In her capacious pantry, there's always a can of Egyptian brown beans on-hand to eat mashed with hard-boiled eggs, and at Rosh Hashanah the family has black-eyed peas, a symbol of plenty, along with leek or spinach omelets.

Stuffed grape leaves with "sour" apricot sauce is another of her special dishes, as is shoulder of lamb stuffed with artichokes, and *hamud* with celery, potatoes, mint and lemon. On Friday nights, she usually makes sofrito chicken, called by her 6 children and 15 grandchildren, "chicken and chips," or she cooks the chicken from the soup in the oven with chickpeas and cumin. "Our chicken soup is served with vermicelli – NO BALLS! I suppose I can manage to eat chopped liver about once a year, but NEVER chopped herring, I simply can't abide the smell or taste."

MAKE the filling by mixing the ingredients together using your hands, then cover and set aside in the fridge.

PREHEAT the oven to 350°F.

PEEL the onions and top and tail them.

MAKE a vertical slit down one side all the way through to the center.

PLACE the onions in boiling water and simmer for 10–15 minutes until tender (or you can microwave them instead).

REMOVE, drain and cool. Each individual layer will now separate easily.

FILL each onion petal/layer with a walnut-sized oval of the filling.

ROLL up each one and place snugly in a single layer in a shallow stovetop casserole dish, seam side down to keep them from unrolling. (You can stuff any remaining onion petals in the gaps, although the rice will expand during cooking, which will help keep them in place.)

MIX the sauce ingredients together and pour over the stuffed onions. Cover with an ovenproof plate to prevent the onions from unrolling.

BRING to a gentle boil, then cook in the oven for 1–1½ hours, by which time the rice will have absorbed nearly all the liquid (if necessary, add a little extra water).

REMOVE from the oven and baste with any remaining liquid and, if desired, grill briefly to glaze the tops an attractive golden brown.

SERVE hot or at room temperature.

MAKES ABOUT 20 STUFFED ONION PETALS, DEPENDING ON THE SIZE OF THE ONIONS
3 large onions

FILLING
1 lb lean ground beef
 or lamb
½ cup plus 1 tbsp washed
 Basmati rice
1 tsp allspice or *baharat*
 (available in Middle Eastern
 stores)
1 tsp ground cinnamon
salt and pepper
1 tsp vegetable oil

SAUCE
2–3 tbsp pomegranate
 (or tamarind) molasses
2–3 tbsp brown sugar
juice of 2 lemons
⅞ cup water
2 tbsp olive oil

Keftes de prasah
Turkish meat and leek patties

Meatballs are ubiquitous throughout the Mediterranean and Middle East, but Sephardi housewives would often add chopped vegetables to stretch the meat as a way of feeding a large family on a small budget. Unusually, these keftes are first dipped in matzo meal or flour then egg, rather than the other way around. They are often served at Pesach, as leeks were one of the seven foods the Israelites yearned for during the Exodus.

SERVES 4

1 lb 2 oz leeks (this may seem a lot, but trust me)

1 lb 2 oz ground beef

2 eggs, beaten

4 tbsp fine matzo meal

nutmeg, salt and white pepper

½ cup chopped walnuts (optional)

medium matzo meal or all-purpose flour, for coating

vegetable oil, for shallow frying

lemon wedges, to serve

FINELY chop the white parts of the leeks (reserve the dark green leaves for use in soups or stews) and steam until soft. Let cool and then squeeze out as much water as possible.

MIX the cooked leeks with the beef, half the egg, the matzo meal, a little nutmeg and seasonings and walnuts (if using) and combine well by hand or pulse in a food processor.

SHAPE into smallish, flattish burgers.

DREDGE with medium matzo meal, then dip into the remaining egg.

FRY in a little oil for 4–5 minutes on each side until brown. Drain on paper towel and serve with lemon wedges.

Grandma Annie Friedman's sweet & sour meatballs

The grandma in question is that of my friend Ruth Kaitiff's husband Leon (are you following me?), who was born in 1905 in the UK into a Romanian family from Bessarabia. The recipe for *essig fleisch* was handed down through the generations, although it was originally made with the wings and giblets of soup hens. Ruth remembers that when she first got married, Annie told her, "Darling, this you gotta learn how to make!"

SERVES 4

MEATBALLS

1 lb ground beef

1 onion, grated

1 small potato, grated

½ cup fine matzo meal

salt and pepper

SAUCE

1 large onion

2 tbsp cane syrup

2½ cups water

2 heaping tbsp long-grain rice

2 tbsp tomato paste or 2–3 fresh tomatoes (skinned and seeded)

handful of seedless raisins

juice of 1 lemon, or to taste

1 heaping tsp ground cinnamon

½ tsp salt

pinch of pepper

MAKE the meatballs by mixing all the ingredients together. Shape into small balls and set aside.

MAKE the sauce by cutting the onion into quarters then into slices and put them into "a strong pan" with the syrup. Cook slowly for about 30 minutes until the onion has caramelized, but keep stirring to prevent it burning. When it's a nice, rich golden color, add the water and bring to a boil. Add the rice, tomato paste, raisins, lemon juice, cinnamon and seasonings. Adjust to taste.

ADD the meatballs, bring back to a boil, turn down the heat and simmer, covered, for a long, long time (that means several hours) until the sauce becomes thick and jammy. Turn the meatballs over at some point so they can absorb the sauce on all sides.

RIGHT: SWEET & SOUR MEATBALLS

Iraqi beet kubba
Beef and beet dumplings

A recipe from Shoshana Keret of Antwerp, Netherlands, who shares her passion for kubba with all other Jews of Iraqi origin. They can take on many colors depending on the vegetables with which they are cooked, but the purple-red that comes from beets is particularly beautiful against the white of the rice that always accompanies it. Shoshana cuts the beets into small pieces, but it can also be grated for equally good effect.

**MAKES 20 KUBBA
(THESE ARE QUITE LARGE, SO
ALLOW ABOUT 3 PER PERSON)**

SAUCE
⅞ cup lemon juice
5 tbsp sugar
salt and pepper
1½ quarts water
1 lb 2 oz beets,
   cooked and cut into
   1¼-inch pieces

SHELL
1 cup plus 2 tbsp fine semolina
¼ tsp salt
⅞ cup water

FILLING
7 oz ground beef
3½ oz onions, grated and
   drained
1 tbsp finely chopped parsley
2 tsp vegetable oil, if the meat
   is very lean
salt and pepper, to taste

MAKE the sauce by combining the lemon juice, sugar and seasonings with the water; stir and boil for 5 minutes. Add the beets and cook for 5 minutes more. Adjust the seasoning to taste, and remove the beets with a slotted spoon. Set aside.

MAKE the shell by mixing the semolina and salt with the water and leave for 5 minutes to soak. Shape the mixture into 20 balls. (You may need a little more or less water than stated, so go cautiously and trust your judgement.)

MAKE the filling by mixing the meat with the onions, parsley, oil (if used) and seasonings. Shape into 20 balls.

WET your hands with cold water and put a semolina ball into the palm of your hand. Create a depression with your thumb and put a meatball into the center. Close the semolina ball around the meatball.

REHEAT the sauce and carefully lower each kubbe into the pan so they are covered by the liquid. Simmer for 10 minutes, then add the beets and cook for another 15 minutes. They will start to float when cooked.

Lahma bi ma'ala
Syrian "meat in the frying pan"

A family recipe from Denise Margolis, who grew up in "Little Syria," a Sephardi oasis in the genteel world of south Manchester, England. She remembers how much of the food she enjoyed was laboriously made in huge quantities by all the women of the household. As she emphasized, "Kibbe, for example – well, you can't just make half a dozen of them. In any case, there's a real skill to making them. It was a question of who had the longest, thinnest fingers. If they're not properly made, well, they can be simply VILE!"

The food at Denise's home was a mix of Syrian, Lebanese and Egyptian: *ful medames*; chickpea and dried fava bean fritters; navy bean soup with fried onions; stuffed breast of lamb with ground beef, rice and fresh fava beans; chicken soup with chickpeas; pickled eggplants and turnips. On Friday nights there would be meat sambusak; tomato soup with rice, celery and small meatballs; chicken sofrito with fried potatoes and mushrooms, or chicken stuffed with ground beef. Lots of stuffed things – carrots, onions, grape leaves, zucchini, eggplant and more, each with their own spicing and recipe. At every meal there was rice with vermicelli, and fresh fruit.

"Flat bread was topped with minced meat, pine nuts and tomato purée, eaten rolled up. The store cupboard would be full of olives, rice, beans and lentils. There was always tabbouleh and yogurt with parsley, cucumber and ice cubes served with *mejadarra* (rice and lentils). Sweetmeats included baklava and *atayif* – a loose yeast pancake topped with pistachios, sugar and cinnamon, or stuffed with cheese and egg." Her mother also made *harebi*, round shortbread bracelets "clasped" with a pistachio, or *ma'amoul* stuffed with pistachios or dates.

"This recipe," Denise says, "can also be made with pieces of meat, but we prefer it with mince. It was traditionally made in a frying pan on top of the stove, hence the name, but I think it's better to use a casserole. It's one of those recipes where, if you tell people what's in it before they eat it, they'll say they don't like it. My son-in-law hates aubergines (eggplant), but he likes this – so I don't tell him what's in it!"

PREHEAT the oven to 300°F.

FRY the onion in the oil in a large frying pan over medium heat, for a few minutes until it starts to soften. Add the beef and fry until it changes color.

STIR in the tomatoes, tomato paste, lemon juice, sugar, allspice and salt. Keep the mixture bubbling on a low heat, then add the eggplant, zucchini and gooseberries (if using). The latter give a lovely sour-sweet flavor but, if used, add less lemon. "TASTE IT – it should be spicy and lemony but not too sharp."

PLACE the potatoes in the bottom of a large casserole dish, then top with the beef. Cover and bake for 2–3 hours, until the potatoes are soft and the eggplant and zucchini have practically disappeared. "They're there to add flavor to the meat but it's not necessary to see them." If desired, lower the temperature more and cook longer – it won't do any harm.

SERVE with Syrian rice and vermicelli (see below).

SERVES 4	salt
1 large onion, grated	1 large eggplant, peeled and chopped
1–2 tbsp vegetable oil	
1 lb ground beef	2 zucchini, peeled and chopped
14 oz can tomatoes	8 oz gooseberries (optional)
5 oz can tomato paste	2 lb 4 oz potatoes,
juice of 2 lemons	thickly sliced
1 tsp sugar	
1 tsp ground allspice	

Syrian rice & vermicelli

"We had this with almost every meal – it padded everything out."

1 cup and 2 tbsp long-grain or Basmati rice	2 tbsp oil or chicken fat
	3¾ cups water
4 handfuls crushed vermicelli	1 tbsp salt

PREHEAT the oven to 350°F.

WASH the rice in a sieve until the water runs clear.

FRY the vermicelli in the oil in an ovenproof pan. "The second it changes color, TAKE IT OFF THE STOVE!" Add the water right away and then the rice and salt.

BRING to a boil, stir and cover. Put in the oven for a good hour.

WHEN it's cooked, the vermicelli rises to the top, so give it a stir to mix it back in again.

As Denise says, "The grains are always separate, never clog up – and if you want you can just heat it up again."

By the waters of Babylon…

AND GOD TOLD THE EXILED JEWS IN BABYLONIA "I WILL TAKE THE CHILDREN OF
ISRAEL… AND BRING THEM INTO THEIR OWN LAND." EZEKIEL 37:21

"How long do you stay?"
"What is your address?"
"Where will you travel?"
"Why are you here?"
The questions from the inscrutable, no-nonsense immigration officer came thick
and fast. Despite the beach babe looks, this was one sugar cookie with a very hard crust.
I explained I had come to do research for a Jewish cookbook.
A long, questioning look.
Then, a broad, beautiful smile.
"So, you want I should give you a recipe?"
Welcome to Israel.

One day in 1969, shortly after the Iraqi government publicly hanged 11 members of the Baghdad
Jewish community following show trials that had falsely accused them of spying, one of Josie
Shamash Smith's cousins, an affluent businessman, went home and dressed his family in three sets
of clothing. He slammed the door shut on the house and all its contents, left his car in the driveway
and set out across the country to make contact with Kurdish insurgents who were able to smuggle
the family across the border.

They were among the last to leave Baghdad, a city that had at one time been one fifth Jewish and
where the Jewish presence dates back over 2,500 years. In fact, there were Jews in Iraq long before it
was an Arab or a Muslim country. In 1948, the community numbered 150,000; in September 2002,
there were said to be only 38, mostly elderly, Jews left in Baghdad, plus a handful more in Kurdish
northern Iraq.

Josie's own grandparents had left Iraq much earlier in the 20th century to become cotton
merchants in the UK, part of a family firm that had branches as far away as India and Japan; many
more, however, were forced to flee after a brutal pro-Nazi pogrom in 1941. Others were permitted
to leave in 1950 but had to forfeit all their homes, businesses and savings. Between 1949 and 1951,
104,000 Iraqi Jews were evacuated in Operations Ezra and Nehemia, to be housed in temporary
refugee camps in Israel until they could be absorbed and resettled in the fledgling state. Twenty
thousand more were smuggled out via Iran. The situation continued to deteriorate: in a decade there
is unlikely to be a single Jew left in the country.

Josie is part of a huge network – a vast clan of Shamash and Dellal families whose inter-relations
and connections are as intricate as a Talmudic debate. Her father alone had something like 100 first

> "Whenever I went to my grandmother's house there was always a wonderful smell of Basmati rice combined with onion. Scents are so evocative – the smell of rice and fried onions still reminds me of her."

CLOCKWISE FROM TOP CENTER:
KURDISH-JEWISH IMMIGRANT;
PICKING AVOCADOS; EATING
FALAFELS; SUKKOT IN ISRAEL

cousins. A small, framed part of the tangled branches of the family tree hangs on the wall of her welcoming home in Rehovot, a bright, bustling town famed as the seat of the world-renowned Weizman Institute. Josie, a mathematician, however, is the product of a "mixed marriage" – an Iraqi father and Ashkenazi mother – and is herself married to another mathematician, a convert of Armenian-German heritage. As Stu chips in, "A lot of Josie's Iraqi cooking has similarities to the Armenian cooking I grew up with – apart from the lamb with yogurt which, of course, is not on the menu these days!"

Josie's paternal grandfather had already established himself in Manchester, England, when the family decided to "import" a bride for him. Lulu Dellal had just finished at the Alliance school in Baghdad and had ambitions to study in Paris. According to Josie, however, "She was just told one day she was going to get married and that was that. In those days, all the girls had their marriages arranged for them at a young age and were expected to have lots of children. She was sent across the desert to Alexandria on donkeys and camel trains, with her gold and jewels concealed about her for fear of being robbed. On arrival, she did an extraordinary thing – and sent all her jewelry back to Baghdad. I think it was her form of personal protest, but she traveled on to England by boat, where she was finally met by my grandfather. As she told the tale, he bought her a chocolate bar from a machine at Victoria station – and won her heart!"

When the cotton business crashed, however, in the late 1920s, her grandparents lost everything and ended up moving to Bridlington (England), where they opened a fancy goods shop. "As the only Jewish family in Bridlington, it was pretty lonely for them." Josie reflected. Her father, however, became a research chemist and moved to London, where he met her mother, who was of Lithuanian and Polish ancestry. "It provoked the most enormous row," she recalled. "My father was expected to marry one of his cousins, and all the Iraqis were absolutely horrified he was going to marry an Ashkenazi. Happily, my grandmother Lulu descended in great style down from Bridlington, with a huge bottle of perfume for my mother and silenced all opposition. The thing about Iraqi Jews is not only do they think they are the most superior in the world, but the Baghdadis think they are the best of the lot!"

Josie's late mother learned to incorporate Iraqi dishes into her own Anglo-Jewish repertoire of gefilte fish and apple pie. Festival customs became quite mixed. "At the Passover seder, for example, we would have two sorts of haroset, an Ashkenazi one and an Iraqi one made from dates, which took forever to make. It was date syrup that you cooked and squeezed through muslin, cooked and squeezed over and over again and ate with skinned ground almonds. But it went the other way as well; our Iraqi cousins would come to us to break their fast after Yom Kippur and so learned to eat herring!"

At Rosh Hashanah, the family would have both apple and honey as well as jam made from apples flavored with rosewater. "You end up with whole, translucent pieces of apple in amber-colored jam; it's very, very good." Josie's aunt Simcha used to make huge platters of her speciality: *m'hasha*, an immense range of stuffed vegetables. "It took great patience. We would all wait for her to come to London to make this every year.

"My grandmother rarely baked anything sweet. Nevertheless, at her house there were always pastries that been made by cousins and aunts. She taught my mother a recipe for yeast pastries stuffed with dates, *ba'ba tamar*, but usually she just cooked on top of the stove and used her oven for storing boxes of biscuits!" A great-aunt was known for her layered dish of spinach, eggs and cheese, and Josie's father, too, had his own speciality, learned from his mother. Passed on to Josie and her siblings, it is a thick, solid omelet with tomato, parsley and cheese, cooked a little in a frying pan and then put under the broiler. It was eaten for breakfast in England, and now for supper in Israel, where the family has lived since making aliyah in 1968.

Another of Lulu's dishes was semolina paste kubba, cooked in either a lemon and tomato sauce with zucchini, carrot and onion, or in a beet and lemon sauce. Other dishes she passed on included a lovely lemony chicken soup, *tabit* (chicken and rice with lemon juice and tomatoes), *shifta* (beef kebab made with onions and lots of parsley), and meatballs fried with rice. Her main speciality, however, was meat with *bamiya* (okra). "It's excellent for Shabbat as it can sit for quite a while on a hot plate. Of course, when Lulu first came to the UK, you couldn't get fresh okra. They were bought dried on cotton and you'd have to soak them for hours to do this recipe which, like everything in the Iraqi kitchen, starts with a fried onion! Whenever I went to my grandmother's house there was always a wonderful smell of Basmati rice combined with onion. Scents are so evocative – the smell of rice and fried onions still reminds me of her."

Baghdad beef with okra

SERVES 8

vegetable oil, for frying

1 large onion, chopped

2 lb 4 oz fore shank beef, cut into large cubes

3–4 carrots, peeled and chopped

2–3 tomatoes, chopped

2–3 zucchini, chopped (or pieces of peeled pumpkin)

salt and pepper

juice of 1 lemon

1 tsp apple pie spice

1 can of tomato paste

1 tsp sugar

4 oz fresh or frozen okra

HEAT a little oil in a stovetop casserole dish and fry the onion until soft, then add the meat and fry until nice and brown.

COVER with water and add the carrots, tomatoes and zucchini (or pumpkin), salt and pepper. The water should just cover the ingredients. Simmer for 2–3 hours, adding water as necessary.

ADD the lemon juice, apple pie spice, tomato paste and sugar – add more, if desired – the aim is to get a good lemony-sweet balance. Add a little more water and then the okra. Cook for at least another hour until the sauce is thick and rich, and the meat so tender it falls apart.

SERVE with rice, either plain or cooked with fried onions (of course!), and/or with tomato paste to color the rice salmon-pink.

Lulu would make this more like a soup – everyone was served the stew as a soup in a bowl, with a huge plate of rice on which you would spoon the meat and vegetables.

Fit for a Queen

According to Molly Bar-David in *The Israeli Cook Book*, there is a legend that King Solomon ordered 100 dishes to welcome the Queen of Sheba. The King's chef could only think of 99, so went in search of a new ingredient. In the fields, he saw the okra pod for the first time and named it *bamia* for *Ben-Maiyah*, which means "the hundredth."

"Let all who are hungry come and eat." PASSOVER HAGGADAH

Cholent

Since lighting a fire on the Sabbath is prohibited, this one-pot stew was put into the oven on Friday afternoon, left on the lowest heat overnight and eaten warm the next day.

As ever with Jewish cooking, there is no single recipe: Indeed, cholent is not so much a recipe as a philosophy that relates to the Talmudic injunction to "hide or bury the hot things" or cover the hot food in preparation for the Sabbath.

Sometimes a huge dumpling is cooked with the cholent. It is called a *ganef* or thief, because the dough "steals" the succulent flavors from the other ingredients, and emerges fat and rich from the pot.

SERVES 6

1 cup dried beans, soaked overnight and drained
3 lb 5 oz brisket, in large cubes
3 onions, chopped
1 garlic clove, chopped
6 tbsp barley or kasha
2 lb 4 oz potatoes, sliced
2 bay leaves
salt and white pepper

GET out the largest, heaviest pot you possess.
BUILD up layers of ingredients, adding salt and pepper as you go, and finishing with a layer of potatoes.
BARELY cover with boiling water and bring to a boil (to cook overnight, it will need more water). Cover with aluminum foil, then a lid, and leave on a very low heat or in a slow cooker – and just forget it for the rest of the day. (Alternatively, put the dish in an oven preheated to 375°F, then turn down to 250°F.)
THERE'S no need to go stirring it up – it will merge into a dense, comforting (or maybe discomforting, depending on the state of your digestion) mass of its own divine accord.

If desired, cholent can be made in advance, so the fat can be discarded, then reheated – but somehow that seems like cheating. The whole point of cholent (or one of them) is to make you feel you've got lead in your boots, a stomach like a bloated bladder and enough inner heating to render you comatose for the rest of the snowy Lithuanian Shabbes afternoon.

Orisa

Although Giselle Sinyor now lives in London, she was brought up in Gibraltar. This recipe, which is of medieval origin, came from her Ceuta grandmother, and is an alternative to *dfina*, another Sephardi Sabbath stew of meat, chickpeas and sweet potatoes.

Quantities are flexible. The most important thing is to have a big, strong pot, but it's a recipe that can come out a bit different every time. As Giselle said when she gave it to me, "Sometimes it seems to work best when I'm in a hurry and I just chuck everything in together – this week, for instance, it came out fabulous, but don't ask me why!"

SERVES 6

1 large onion, chopped
vegetable oil
1 tbsp brown sugar (optional)
3 lb 5 oz stewing beef, cubed
2¼ cups whole wheat berries, soaked overnight and drained
1 whole, unpeeled head of garlic
6 large potatoes, cut into chunks
3 sweet potatoes, cut into chunks
fore shank bone (optional, but good)
1 tbsp sweet paprika
½ tbsp hot paprika (optional)
salt and pepper, to taste
6 eggs in their shell, washed*

FRY the onion in enough oil to cover the base of the pan until it softens and turns light gold. If desired, add some brown sugar to help the onion caramelize and to add extra flavor.
ADD the meat in batches and fry until it starts to brown.
ADD the whole wheat berries, head of garlic, potatoes, fore shank bone, paprika and seasonings. Arrange the eggs around the top of the stew.
COVER with water, bring to a boil and either simmer, covered, on top of the stove or in a very low oven for 6–7 hours or overnight. You may need to top off with water as the wheat will absorb a lot of liquid. If desired, it can be left on a *blech* or hot plate, or in a slow cooker for Sabbath. As Giselle says, "Some people like it very dry, others like a bit more juice; either way, the longer you leave it to simmer, the better." When you serve the orisa, you can either discard or squeeze out the garlic from the clove, as you like.

*The eggs can be pre-boiled and shelled before being added to the casserole if preferred, in order to avoid peeling eggs on Sabbath.

Sauerbraten

Slow-cooked brisket is a favorite Jewish holiday dish; inexpensive, easy to prepare in advance and great for leftover sandwiches with pickles. There are as many versions as there are Jewish cooks, but this German-Austrian classic, with a slightly tart edge from the vinegar, is particularly good.

SERVES 6–8
4 lb 8 oz brisket
2 large onions, chopped
4–5 tbsp vegetable oil
4 tbsp margarine (optional)
2 tbsp all-purpose flour
    (optional)

MARINADE
1 quart red wine
4 tbsp wine vinegar
2 large onions, chopped
2 large carrots, chopped
2 celery sticks, chopped
1 leek, chopped
2 bay leaves
4 cloves
6 peppercorns
4 allspice or juniper berries
1 tsp ground ginger
1 tsp salt

MAKE the marinade by mixing all the ingredients together in a pan, bringing to a boil then letting cool. Pour over the meat, cover and refrigerate for 3 days. If the meat is not completely covered by the liquid, turn daily.

PREHEAT the oven to 325°F.

DRAIN the meat and dry it, reserving the marinade.

FRY the onions in the oil in a large stovetop casserole dish, until brown. Add the beef, turning so it browns on all sides. Add the marinade, bring to a boil and cover the casserole dish tightly.

BAKE for 2½–3 hours, turning the meat now and then. If necessary, add a little water. Remove the lid for the last 15 minutes.

REMOVE the beef and strain the gravy. Skim off the fat from the liquid. The juices are delicious just like this, but if you prefer a thicker gravy, melt the margarine in a saucepan over a low heat and blend in the flour. Stir slowly until light brown, then gradually add the marinade liquid, stirring until thick and smooth.

SLICE the meat – it should be almost soft enough to cut with a spoon – and serve with the gravy, red cabbage, dumplings, noodles or spätzle.

Gedempte fleisch

Gedempte, which means to "braise very, very slowly until it's falling to bits," is one of the favorite techniques of Ashkenazi cooking. My late mother, when not frying, was gedempting: meat, chicken, potatoes, vegetables. She could even gedempte a can of peas. In part, this was an ingrained fear of – God forbid – food not being thoroughly cooked, but it was also because this method best suits most kosher cuts of meat.

This recipe was her usual way with beef, apart from the use of tomatoes which, I think, she instinctively regarded with the same suspicion her Polish ancestors did when they were first introduced to Eastern Europe and were thought – heaven forbid – to contain blood.

Nor did she use paprika or garlic (far too fancy-schmancy); in fact, this isn't her recipe at all, but mine. And I wish she were here to eat it with me today.

SERVES 6–8
4 lb 8 oz brisket or
    similar cut
4 tbsp oil or schmaltz
3 onions, sliced
1 celery stick, sliced
2 carrots, sliced

3 garlic cloves, chopped
4 bay leaves
2 tsp paprika
5 oz tomatoes, skinned and
    chopped
salt and pepper
1¼ cups water

HEAT the oil in a heavy, stovetop casserole dish and brown the brisket on all sides.

ADD the remaining ingredients, bring to a boil, then simmer for 2–2½ hours until the meat is very tender. Baste occasionally and add a little more water, if necessary, to keep the beef from burning.

Hungarian stuffed breast of veal

A recipe, adapted, from Marguerite Zollmann of Antwerp, Netherlands. She learned it from her mother, the pistachios are her own touch.

SERVES 6

1 lb 2 oz ground meat (veal, turkey or chicken)

2 eggs, beaten

2 pieces stale bread, steeped in water, squeezed dry and shredded

2 small onions, finely chopped

1 garlic clove, crushed

2 tbsp mixed peppercorns

3 tbsp vegetable oil

"handful" of finely chopped celery, leeks, carrots and pistachios

1 breast of veal, about 2 lb 4 oz ("Ask the butcher to make a pocket, then when you get home open it up further with a little knife as the butcher never makes it quite big enough – but take care not to pierce the meat")

2 hard-boiled eggs (optional)

paprika, for rubbing

1 onion, chopped

1 tsp cornstarch, dissolved in a little water

stock powder, for the gravy

PREHEAT the oven to 350°F.

MIX the ground meat, eggs, bread, one of the onions, garlic, half the peppercorns and most of the oil to make a stuffing, then add the finely chopped celery, leeks, carrots and pistachios.

STUFF the veal (you can also add 2 whole hard-boiled eggs, if there's enough room). Sew up with a big needle. Brown on both sides in a little oil in a heavy casserole dish and rub on some paprika (if you put it on before you brown the meat, it burns).

REMOVE the veal from the casserole dish and set aside. Soften the other chopped onion in the casserole dish, then add the remaining peppercorns. Pour in a little water and lay the veal over the onions.

COVER and cook in the oven for about 2 hours, basting regularly and adding more water, if necessary. Remove the lid for the final 20 minutes to allow the meat to color.

TOWARD the end of cooking, add the cornstarch and a little stock powder to make a gravy (perhaps with a drop of sherry).

Shashlik

Grilling meat on an open fire goes back to biblical times. To this day, barbecues are an Israeli passion, and everyone is a barbecue maven. In summer, small fires dot the hills, parks and beaches, or any open space where it is possible to rig up a small portable grill. As a national culinary sport, it is second only to falafel munching.

Za'atar is one of the nation's favorite dried spice mixes, although quality and composition varies widely. Based on hyssop, wild thyme, dried sumac, salt and toasted sesame seeds, sometimes also with oregano, marjoram or savory, it adds a herbal, nutty edge to marinades, salad dressings, yogurt, grilled fish or meat. It is also good to sprinkle, together with a little olive oil, on to hot pita bread.

Grind your own using 4 tablespoons lightly toasted sesame seeds, 3 tablespoons dried thyme or oregano, 2 tablespoons of sumac and salt, to taste.

SERVES 4

2 tbsp lemon juice

1 large clove garlic, finely chopped

2 tsp za'atar

salt and pepper

5 tbsp olive oil

1 lb 10 oz shoulder lamb, trimmed of excess fat and cut into 2-inch cubes

3 small red, yellow and green peppers, each cut into 8 pieces

2 small onions, each cut into 8 pieces

HEAT Mix the lemon juice with the garlic and seasonings, then slowly whisk in the olive oil until the marinade starts to thicken. Add the lamb and coat well with the marinade. Chill for at least 6 hours, preferably overnight, turning from time to time.

DRAIN the lamb, reserving the marinade. Thread the meat onto metal or pre-soaked wooden skewers, interspersing with pieces of pepper and onion. Brush with some marinade.

COOK for about 12–15 minutes under a very hot, pre-heated broiler or grill for a few minutes longer on an oiled rack over glowing coals, basting with the remaining marinade.

FAR LEFT: GEORGIAN BREAD;
LEFT: MOROCCAN TAGINES

Lamalo lamb tagine with almonds & prunes

Lamalo means "Why not?" in Hebrew, and when the idea of opening a stylish, modern Mediterranean restaurant in the heart of Antwerp's diamond district came to Israeli-born Ika Zaken and Yitzhak Cohen, that's just what they thought. The menu draws considerably on Jewish Moroccan recipes from their own families, but presented with considerable sophistication in a setting where every detail has been carefully considered, from the hand-cut salads to the specially commissioned pottery. Middle Eastern bread is baked to order, the walls are lined with homemade pickles, and Ika's wife makes the most delicious pâtisserie. Customers range from large blonde Flemish ladies who look as if they have stepped from the frame of a Rubens painting, to diamond dealers, tourists and religious Jews. Oh, yes, it's a kosher restaurant as well. So, why not?

SERVES 6

2 lb 4 oz lamb shoulder or
    neck, cut into pieces
salt and black pepper
6 tbsp vegetable oil
2 onions, finely chopped
3 garlic cloves, finely chopped
1 tsp ground ginger
1 tsp saffron powder
1 tbsp honey
1 tbsp ground cinnamon
2½ cups pitted prunes
10 black peppercorns tied in a
    cheesecloth bag
6 cups toasted blanched
    almonds

CUT the lamb shoulder into pieces – neck should already be in slices on the bone. Season with salt and pepper.

HEAT the oil in a stovetop casserole dish and brown the pieces of lamb. Remove with a slotted spoon and set aside.

GENTLY sauté the onions for 10 minutes, then add the garlic. When soft, add the ginger, saffron, 1 teaspoon of salt, and the lamb.

ADD just enough water to cover the lamb. Bring to a boil then reduce the heat to a simmer. Cover and cook until the lamb is tender, at least 45 minutes (although it will not spoil if cooked longer).

ADD the honey, cinnamon, prunes and peppercorns and cook for another 15–20 minutes. Remove the bag of peppercorns, and garnish with the toasted almonds before serving with rice or couscous.

FAR LEFT: MATZO
"SANDWICHES";
LEFT: ISRAELI MATZO
RIGHT: MSOKI

Msoki

Tunisian lamb casserole for Passover

You can use any variety of vegetable, such as peas, cabbage, fennel, artichokes, turnips and so on. Sometimes, "les Tuns" also add meatballs or *osban*, a spicy sausage made from veal and tripe.

Serve with rice if a) you're Tunisian, b) you're not Jewish or c) it's not Passover. Otherwise serve with – more matzo!

SERVES 6

3 tbsp olive oil

1¾ cups water

1 tbsp tomato paste

2 lb 4 oz lamb shoulder, cubed and seasoned with salt, pepper and 1 tsp paprika

2 onions, sliced

1 celery stalk, sliced

2 carrots, diced

6 garlic cloves, chopped

1 tsp ground cinnamon

1 cup fava beans, shelled

1 leek, sliced

4 fresh artichoke hearts cut into chunks or 3½ oz frozen or a 14 oz undrained can of artichoke hearts

2 zucchini, sliced

8 oz fresh spinach

2 tbsp each chopped fresh parsley, cilantro and dill

1 tbsp fresh mint, chopped

harissa or cayenne, to taste

salt and pepper

2 sheets matzo, broken into small pieces

WHISK the oil, water and tomato paste and pour into a large casserole dish. Add the lamb, onions, celery, carrots, garlic and cinnamon. Bring to a boil, cover and simmer for 30 minutes. Stir from time to time.

ADD the fava beans, leek, artichokes and zucchini. Bring back to a boil, cover again and simmer for at least another 30 minutes until the meat is tender.

ADD the spinach, allow to cook down then add the fresh herbs, leaving some for garnish. Add harissa or cayenne.

PLACE the pieces of matzo on top of the stew and press down gently so they start to soften. Sprinkle with the remaining herbs before serving.

The Bread of Affliction

"And they baked unleavened cakes of the dough which they brought forth out of Egypt, for it was not leavened: because they were thrust out of Egypt and could not tarry, neither had they prepared for themselves any victual." EXODUS 12:39

Pareve

Chopped herring | Smoked salmon citrus salad | Perez family bulgur & chickpea salad | Potato & tomato curry | Tunisian brik with tuna & potatoes | Tunisian pepper & tomato salad | Carrot tzimmes | Raya Wimmer's Siberian tzimmes | Potato latkes | Potato kugel | Vegetable kugel | Jerusalem kugel | South African "Danish" herring | Rubens family potato chremslach | Lithuanian pickled halibut | Fish in Red Sea sauce | Italian tuna & rice salad | Spicy Libyan fish | Fresh sardines stuffed with herbs | Egyptian fish with lemon | Grilled trout Kinneret-style | Anglo-Jewish gefilte fish | Dutch fish cakes | Moroccan fish boulettes | Moroccan fish with chickpeas and cilantro | Sophie's poppy seed torte | Almond cake | Carrot cake from Aargau | Sponge cake | Easy apple strudel | Zena's lekach | Linzertorte | Chocolate babka | Sfenz | Orecchi di Aman | Frou-frou chalet | Pineapple fritters à la Célestine | Old-fashioned sweet carrot kugel | Lokshen kugel | Biscochos de huevo | Marunchinos |Mandelbrot | Zimtsterne | Jennifer Hyman's beet jam

Chopped herring

A topping of chopped hard-boiled egg helps but does not succeed in disguising the dismal gray color of chopped herring; nor does the taste, frankly, appeal to everyone. You either love or hate the pungent, almost savage taste. It may well be something genetically inherited. Novices are allowed to add some sugar, but most true Ashkenazi stomachs need no such refinement.

SERVES 6

1 lb 2 oz jar
of pickled herring fillets
(instead of traditional
salt herring)
4 hard-boiled eggs

½ mild white onion
1 small apple, peeled
2 tbsp ground almonds
1 tbsp lemon juice
white pepper
1 tsp sugar (optional)

DRAIN the herring and rinse well. Dry on paper towel.
BRIEFLY pulse all ingredients except for one of the eggs in a processor (although I sometimes still use my vintage *hachmesser*, the two-handled chopper and curved board once kept specially for herring.)
THE chopped herring should not be too pasty; it needs some texture.
TASTE for seasoning and add a little extra sugar, if desired. Let mature for a few hours before using.
SCATTER with the reserved, chopped hard-boiled egg before serving with matzo, crackers, rye bread or challah as a *forspeise* (appetizer).

"All the pleasures of the world are in my hands, white bread, a drop of brandy and herring and other good things to enable the Sabbath, and – not to put it on the same plane – my body, to rejoice."
S.Y. Agnon, Eilu Va'eilu

Smoked salmon citrus salad

This is an instant heritage recipe, based on one I was served at a smart, waterside restaurant when researching my previous book on Sicilian cooking. Jews were expelled from Sicily in 1492 and few traces are left of their presence, so I was wryly amused by this reunion of two traditions.

8 oz smoked salmon torn into
strips (use a mild Jewish
smoke, not a strong oak-
wood smoked salmon)
2 oranges (preferably blood
oranges), peeled, all pith
and membrane removed
and segmented or sliced
2 red onions, finely sliced

3½ oz olives, green
or black (optional)
fresh salad leaves or basil

DRESSING
4 tbsp extra virgin olive oil
2 tbsp lemon juice
salt and black pepper

ARRANGE the smoked salmon, oranges and onions on a large serving dish. Scatter with the salad leaves or basil.
MAKE the dressing by whisking all the ingredients together.
DRIZZLE over the salad and toss gently before serving.

"Where there's smoke, there may be smoked salmon." MODERN JEWISH PROVERB

RIGHT: SMOKED SALMON CITRUS SALAD

Perez family bulgur & chickpea salad

Leah Perez of Montréal told me that the recipe for this simple, pretty salad originally came from a magazine or newspaper many years ago. "I don't even remember which one… the cutting is so old. Although I was born in Montréal, my husband is Moroccan. We met and married in Israel and then came here in 1980. I like to make this salad when we have a family gathering because it is filling, makes a lot and is easy (I double the amounts because we are usually 18 people at the table). My girls like to take the leftovers (if there are any) as a packed lunch to school the next day."

SERVES 8

⅝ cup medium bulgur

½ cup olive or vegetable oil

½ cup lemon juice

salt and pepper

1 bunch scallions, chopped

20 oz can chickpeas, drained

1 bunch parsley, finely chopped

5 oz carrots, grated

SOAK the bulgur according to the package instructions, then drain, squeezing well to get rid of excess moisture.

BEAT the oil, lemon juice and seasonings together and mix into the bulgur.

PUT in the bottom of a glass serving bowl. Layer, in this order, the scallions, chickpeas, parsley and carrots. Cover and chill.

TOSS the salad just before serving.

Potato & tomato curry

An aromatic, gently spiced dish from Norma Suvarna of the Bene Israel community of Bombay.

SERVES 4

3 tbsp vegetable oil

½ tsp mustard seeds

1 medium onion, sliced

½ tsp grated fresh ginger

½ tsp finely chopped garlic

4–5 curry leaves

½ tsp chili powder

3 tomatoes, sliced

salt, to taste

3 potatoes, peeled, boiled and cubed

½ tsp garam masala (either use ready-made or crush together 1 clove, the seeds of 1 cardamom pod, 1-inch cinnamon stick and 7 black peppercorns)

14 fl oz can of coconut milk

FRY the mustard seeds in the oil in a heavy pan until they splutter. Add the onion and fry until it turns transparent.

ADD the ginger, garlic, curry leaves and chili powder and cook for 2 minutes, then add the tomatoes and salt. Fry gently until the tomatoes are soft.

ADD the potatoes and garam masala and stir-fry over a medium heat for 5 minutes. Finally, add the coconut milk and bring to a boil.

REMOVE immediately from the heat.

This is often served with rice cooked in a mixture of thick and thin coconut milk, cloves and green cardamom pods.

LEFT: PEREZ FAMILY BULGUR & CHICKPEA SALAD

Tunisian brik with tuna & potatoes

The Tunisian Jewish community now numbers only around 2,000; although they had enjoyed, for the most part, a relatively peaceful life in the country for many centuries until 1948, over 80,000 subsequently emigrated to either Israel or France. "Les Tuns," however, retain a fierce pride in their culinary traditions and a friendly rivalry with fellow North African Moroccan and Algerian Jews in the ways of the table. Brik are one of the most loved of Tunisian snacks; larger than borekas, and made with a delicate semolina flour pastry called *malsouqa*, they can be either deep-fried or baked. A whole egg is the most distinctive filling (and the most tricky to both make and eat), and there is also a lovely sweet version made with almonds and pine nuts in a honey sauce, but there are any number of variations, including this permutation of two traditional ingredients.

SERVES 8

1 small onion, finely chopped
vegetable oil, for frying
3½ oz canned tuna in olive oil,
    drained and crumbled
3 potatoes, peeled and boiled
1 egg, beaten
1 oz parsley, finely chopped
1 tbsp capers

½ tsp turmeric
pinch of harissa (or more,
    to taste)
salt and pepper
16 sheets phyllo pastry or
    8 sheets brik pastry
egg yolk, for brushing
    (optional)

LIGHTLY fry the onion in a little oil and let cool.

MASH the tuna and potatoes with the rest of the ingredients except the pastry and oil and set aside.

CUT the phyllo pastry into 6-inch squares. Brush a pastry square with oil then place another phyllo square on top – you need 2 layers for each brik unless using special brik pastry.

PLACE a large tablespoon of filling in the center, then either fold to make an oblong or triangular shape. Moisten the edges with water in order to seal the pastry.

DEEP-FRY for a minute at 375°F until golden brown, turning if not completely submerged in the oil, then drain on paper towel. Alternatively, brush with some egg yolk beaten with a little water, and bake in a preheated oven at 350°F for about 30 minutes. Best eaten hot.

Tunisian pepper & tomato salad

La slata mechouia

Every Tunisian cook has their own recipe for this favorite salad, which can be served unadorned, *garni*, as a condiment, or as an appetizer or entrée. Worth making in large amounts, as it keeps well in the fridge.

PER PERSON

1 red pepper and the same
    weight in ripe tomatoes
1 garlic clove, unpeeled
juice of half a lemon
extra virgin olive oil
salt, to taste

OPTIONAL

good quality canned tuna
hard-boiled eggs
black and/or green olives
capers

PREHEAT the oven to 425°F.

ARRANGE the peppers, tomatoes and unpeeled garlic in a baking pan and roast for about 30 minutes until the peppers are blackened in places – turn over at least once.

REMOVE and place the peppers in a sealed plastic bag for 15 minutes to help the skin slide off more easily. Remove the seeds – it helps to have a bowl of cold water at hand as you work so you can keep rinsing your fingers to prevent the seeds sticking to them.

RUB the skin off the tomatoes, and squeeze the garlic pulp from its skin.

PUT all the vegetables on a board and chop into small pieces. Drain off any extra juices.

PLACE the chopped vegetables in a large bowl and season with lemon juice, olive oil and salt.

MIX carefully and chill for at least 3 hours.

SERVE garnished, as desired, with tuna, eggs, olives and capers.

RIGHT: TUNISIAN BRIK WITH TUNA & POTATOES

Carrot tzimmes

Tzimmes (to rhyme with Guinness) is one of the great Ashkenazi dishes served on Sabbath and festivals, especially Rosh Hashanah (for a sweet and prosperous year) and Succoth (to celebrate the fruit of the earth). The word "tzimmes" also means fussy, the overcomplication of a simple situation or to make a big deal of something – not that this relates, in any way, to the rich, melting flavors of this slow-cooked, savory-sweet fruit and vegetable stew. It may apply, however, to the messy storm of controversy that erupts every time Jewish cooks compare notes. So, you don't like my recipe? Sue me!

This is best made the day before it's eaten, to allow the flavors to mellow.

SERVES 6–8

1 large onion, finely chopped

2 tbsp margarine (or schmaltz for a meat meal)

1 lb 2 oz carrots, sliced like coins

1 lb 2 oz sweet potatoes, cut into small pieces

⅝ cup pitted prunes

⅝ cup chopped apricots (the better the quality of the dried fruit, the better the tzimmes)

3 tbsp honey

zest of 1 orange

zest of 1 lemon

juice of 2 oranges and 2 lemons (to make about 1 cup juice)

½ tsp ground cinnamon

a little grated nutmeg

salt and white pepper

SAUTÉ the onion in the margarine in a large pot over a medium heat until tender.

ADD the carrots, sweet potatoes, prunes, apricots, honey, zest, juice, spices and seasoning. Bring to a boil, then reduce the heat to a simmer. Give the pot a good stir, then cover and simmer for about 45 minutes until the carrots and sweet potatoes are tender. Stir occasionally.

TASTE and adjust the seasonings if necessary – it needs to be sweet, but not sickly-sweet.

See, it wasn't such a big production after all – the worst part is peeling the vegetables.

Raya Wimmer's Siberian tzimmes

Raya now lives in Antwerp, Netherlands, but her family came from Nowo-Sibirsk in Siberia, or Nowo-Nikolayevsk as it was called previously. "My great-grandfather received a permit to live in this city after serving in the army of the Tsar for 25 years. It was very unusual because, at that time, Jews were only allowed to live outside the cities. Later, after the Revolution, it became impossible for Jews to practice their religion properly in the big towns, so it was left to the old grandmothers to transmit the traditions through the kitchen. My mother remembers how we would eat tzimmes at the end of each Passover, and we have carried on the tradition. My children now call this recipe 'baba's carrots' (that is Grandma's carrots). I hope that, one day, my grandchildren will ask me also to prepare them, and they will taste the same as they did in Siberia a century earlier."

SERVES 4

2 lb 4 oz carrots, thinly sliced

½ cup sugar

⅓ cup honey

a few pitted prunes

water

salt and pepper

PUT all the ingredients in a heavy cast iron pot. Cover with water, then cover the pot and simmer all day.

STIR occasionally to make sure it's not sticking. Serve warm.

LEFT: CARROT TZIMMES

Potato latkes
Potato pancakes

As all latkologists know, the test of a good latke is the returnability factor – are they so good you want to return for more? Although latkes are eaten year-round, serious, competitive latke-fressing reaches its peak at Hanukkah. The irony, however, is that the potato was unknown in ancient Israel at the time of the oil miracle in the Temple, so the essence of the festival is in the frying, not the potato. Latkes, therefore, can be made with any variety of vegetable, but for most people, the potato will always be at the heart of things. A latke without a potato would be, well, like fancy without the schmancy.

SERVES 4–5 (ABOUT 2–3 LATKES PER PERSON)
2 lb 4 oz baking potatoes, peeled and soaked in cold water until needed
1 onion, grated or finely chopped
¼ cup all-purpose flour or fine matzo meal
1 egg, beaten
salt and white pepper
olive or vegetable oil, for frying

FINELY – or not so finely – grate the potatoes and onion together. (You don't have to go back in time and do this by hand, although there are those who swear by the taste of grated knuckle.)

PUT the grated potato and onion into a colander and squeeze out as much moisture as you can. Or roll in a clean dish towel and wring well to extract the liquid.

MIX the potato and onion with the flour, egg, and seasonings.

HEAT the oil until moderately hot, then shallow-fry large tablespoons of the mixture. Lower the heat to medium, flatten each latke with the back of a spoon and fry for about 5 minutes on each side, flipping over when the edges turn brown. If the heat is too high, the latkes will become dark brown on the outside before they're cooked inside.

DRAIN on brown paper bags (they absorb the oil, leave the latkes crispier and won't stick to the paper).

SERVE hot with sour cream and applesauce, or with corned beef and a sour pickle.

The only drawback to latke-making is you have to keep trying so many to see if you've got them right, you can't eat anything else.

Potato kugel
Potato pudding

To mash or grate, that is the question? And that's even before you get around to deciding whether or not to fry the onions before combining them with the potatoes. We can even argue about whether or not to separate the eggs (but we won't – I'm writing this, not you). Mashed potato kugel has its adherents, but I find grated, along with a touch of modern baking powder, helps prevent the kugel from sinking in your stomach like a stone. Carrot, too, is a bit of a daring addition to this most homely of dishes, but it adds a fleck of color to what can only be described as *shtetl* beige.

SERVES 4–6
1 largish onion, finely chopped
6 largish potatoes (about 2 lb), grated
1 largish carrot (I know, but this is a Jewish recipe), grated
2 eggs, well beaten
½ tsp baking powder
freshly, grated nutmeg
salt and pepper
3–4 tbsp matzo meal
4 tbsp oil (or schmaltz)

PREHEAT the oven to 425°F.

FRY the onion in a little of the oil until soft.

COMBINE with the potatoes and carrot, the eggs, baking powder, seasonings and enough matzo meal to absorb most of the liquid.

PUT the remaining oil in a casserole dish, place in the oven and heat for 5 minutes. CAREFULLY – so you don't burn yourself – remove from the oven and swirl the oil around the sides. Add the potato mixture to the dish and fold it over so it makes contact with the oil on all sides.

BAKE for 10 minutes then reduce the heat to 350°F and bake for 45 minutes until the interior is creamy and the kugel is covered in a crunchy, golden crust – the best part.

Vegetable kugel

SERVES 4–6

10 oz broccoli florets
    or sliced leeks (or a mixture
    of both)

1 large onion, finely chopped

¼ cup margarine, or 3–4 tbsp
    oil (or schmaltz) plus extra
    for drizzling

7 oz carrots, grated

2 tbsp fine matzo meal

2 eggs, lightly beaten with
    1–2 tbsp paprika and plenty
    of salt and pepper

STEAM the broccoli and/or leeks until tender.

SAUTÉ the onions in the margarine in a large frying pan until soft.

STIR in the carrots and cook for another few minutes until they too
soften, and absorb the fat.

ADD the broccoli and take off the heat. Turn the vegetables into a well-
greased, ovenproof casserole dish and then mix in the matzo meal and
seasoned eggs.

DOT OR DRIZZLE the top with a little extra margarine or oil and bake for
30 minutes until the top is crusty and golden-brown (but not burnt!).

CUT into portions, and serve straight from the dish.

Jerusalem kugel

The recipe for this intriguing peppery, caramelized kugel, is said to
have come to Jerusalem in the 18th century with the Gaon of Vilna
and his followers. It has been associated with the ultra-orthodox
area of the city ever since.

SERVES 4–6

9 oz fine noodles or vermicelli

2 eggs

1 cup sugar

1 tsp ground cinnamon

1 tsp black pepper

salt

CARAMEL

⅝ cup vegetable oil

¼ cup sugar

PREHEAT the oven to 350°F.

BOIL the noodles according to the package instructions until al dente.
Drain, rinse in cold water and return to the pot.

HEAT the oil and sugar for the caramel in a small pan, stirring
constantly, for 5–10 minutes. The sugar will go into clumps before it
melts and turns dark brown. Take care, first not to splash yourself with
the hot oil, and second that it doesn't burn – it can happen in a flash.

POUR the hot caramel over the noodles – stand back as it will bubble
up rather fiercely – and stir in well with a wooden spoon. Set aside to
cool slightly.

MIX the eggs, sugar, cinnamon, black pepper and salt to taste, and stir
into the noodles.

TRANSFER to a greased ovenproof dish (about 1½ quarts capacity) and
bake, uncovered, for a good hour until the top of the kugel is crisp
and golden brown.

RUN a knife around the edge of the kugel, turn upside down onto a
heated serving plate, unmold and serve.

Cholent Park

MRS. YENTA GELKOP WAS ENJOYING A WELL-EARNED GLASS OF LEMON TEA WITH
HER DAUGHTER, HINDA LOK, VISITING FROM STAMFORD HILL, LONDON, WHO WAS
ACTING AS IMPROMPTU YIDDISH-ENGLISH INTERPRETER.

Yenta, a survivor of the Lodz Ghetto, is one of those special "yiddishe mommas" whose price, as the saying goes, is above rubies. At 78 years old – *keyn eynhore*! – she was still cooking up a storm in her semi-private restaurant discreetly tucked away in the heart of Antwerp's Jewish quarter, serving stuffed cabbage and potato kugel, gefilte fish and knaidlach and all the stars of the traditional *haimishe* repertoire to a select and loyal group of ultra-orthodox customers – "not customers, friends!" – as she has been doing for almost half a century.

Yenta came to the Netherlands from Poland after the war, and in 1955 opened Restaurant Gelkop. She used to open daily, but now – well, Yenta's getting on a bit, so the restaurant only opens half the week and for special occasions, "but, of course, people still come here for their Shabbes cholent," added Hinda. She explained that the center of Antwerp, sometimes described as the last *shtetl* in Europe, is surrounded by an *eruv*, a symbolic wire enclosure that permits orthodox Jews to carry objects or push strollers, the sort of work normally forbidden on a Sabbath.

Every Saturday, after synagogue, a line forms outside the restaurant to collect the pots of cholent that Yenta has made on Friday and which have been left to cook overnight in the falling heat of a baker's oven. "You won't see this anywhere else in Europe," said Hinda, "It's like we were back in *der heim*! Some have small pots, others have big ones, sometimes, if the pots are very heavy, they have to take them away in little push carts. It's tradition, tradition is at the bottom of everything – you've got to have cholent on Shabbes after *shul*!" And it's tradition, she might well have added, to also have a nice *shlof* (snooze) after the cholent and then a small, restorative stroll in the nearby City Park, locally nicknamed Cholent Park.

So, I asked, was Yenta thinking of retiring? "She's cut down a bit, but what else would she do? It's the days when she doesn't work she starts to feel unwell!" said Hinda affectionately. "Her biggest compliment is when someone says it's just like their mother used to make. That makes her really happy."

Large numbers of Jews arrived in liberal-minded Antwerp from Eastern Europe toward the end of the 19th century, and by the outset of World War II numbered 55,000, but over 30,000 were subsequently deported to the concentration camps. The cosmopolitan, close-knit Jewish population now numbers around 20,000 and the city has some 30 orthodox synagogues, plus a superb choice of kosher restaurants and shops. About a quarter of the community is ultra-orthodox, and there are numerous small Hassidic synagogues and study houses packed into the narrow, congested streets east of the Central Railway Station. This square-cut urban area is also the brilliant, beating heart of Antwerp's renowned diamond trade; even the tram stop is called Diamant. The business was once the sole Yiddish-speaking province of Jewish cutters, polishers and merchants to the extent that the

This square-cut urban area is also the brilliant, beating heart of Antwerp's renowned diamond trade; even the tram stop is called Diamant.

CLOCKWISE FROM TOP CENTER:
ANTWERP CATHEDRAL & CAFES;
THE GROTE MARKT;
BRABO FOUNTAIN & STADHUIS;
THE JEWISH QUARTER;
A TRAM STOP

exchanges closed on Jewish holidays and million-dollar deals were confirmed with simply a wish of *Mazel u'bracha* (luck and blessing). A diamond may be forever, but in recent years the trade has changed its cultural character with an influx of traders from India, Russia and elsewhere.

The city of Antwerp, too, has seen many changes since it burst on to the modern map of Europe as City of Culture. Cobbled streets and trams, fine squares and fountains, beautifully preserved guild houses with gabled roofs, Rubens paintings, a myriad of galleries, smart restaurants and fashion shops give the city a polished veneer. It is indeed a gem of a city, but like all great ports, Antwerp also has a slightly bohemian air, an intangible whiff of impermanence, of comings and goings, of unknown adventure, of new beginnings in new lands.

Many Antwerp Jews arrived here on their way to elsewhere, mostly to the *goldene medine* of New York, but some, such as the Hoffman family from Hungary, stayed. Moishe Hoffman now owns the famous Hoffy's, a kosher restaurant par excellence, and a popular stopping point on tourist tours of Jewish Antwerp.

"From the start, my father felt it important to learn Flemish, to fit in. That is one of the reasons I welcome non-Jewish customers. My parents came to Antwerp after the war to get a US visa. One day my father was waiting for some documentation, and got into conversation with someone who said, 'Why schlep to America? Why not stay here?' He thought about it and decided to stay. And now, every day, he says he's very happy he did!"

Moishe is the eighth of 12 children, and was originally in the diamond trade, but 18 years ago, his father encouraged him to start the small deli that has since become the wonderful restaurant and catering business it is today. To paraphrase the famous saying: you don't have to be Jewish to eat at Hoffy's, but it does help to have a *gezundhe* (healthy) appetite.

Hungarian Jews are legendary cooks, but even so, the cooking at Hoffy's is an eye-opener. "We have to keep evolving the menu. It's very hard in a kosher kitchen, but we do our best." His "best" is a typically modest understatement: a sample platter included tiny eggplants with a spicy tomato stuffing; deep-fried Hungarian cauliflower; Belgian egg and vegetable terrine; chicken with a helzel stuffing; rice with kasha and garlic; chicken kebab with spicy sauce; Belgian braised endive... plus a cucumber ribbon wrapped around a little green salad. "Who says Jewish food isn't healthy?" joked Moishe.

The deli selection on the snaking glass counter is even more mouthwatering, from scarlet peppers stuffed with rice and meat to crisp, golden strudels, chicken with prunes and apricots in rich mahogany hues, tiny stuffed zucchini, noodles sprinkled with nut-brown fried onions, rice with kasha and herbs, lacy potato latkes, kugels galore, a dozen dazzling salads – "That's nothing," Moishe interrupted my reverie, "you should see it on Sunday – there's hardly room for an extra pickle!"

Most of the closely guarded recipes originate with Moishe's mother, but he pays tribute to his long-serving staff. Unlike some notorious Jewish restaurants, where insulting the customer is elevated to an art form, Moishe's attitude is, "it doesn't cost extra to be polite." As their slogan so aptly puts it – at Hoffy's, "You're more than welcome."

South African "Danish" herring

Doreen Zurel now lives in Antwerp, but her maternal grandparents left Lithuania for South Africa around the turn of the 20th century. She remembers her grandmother making this, and says it is popular in the South African Jewish community for festive occasions. "The beauty of it is that you can make it two or three days in advance. No one knows why it's called Danish – but that's the name it always goes by!"

6 cups matjes herring (or salt herring soaked overnight and rinsed)
⅞ cup plus 1 tbsp brown sugar
½ cup vegetable oil
1 cup chopped apple
½ cup chopped onion
½ cup raisins (optional)
1½ cups vinegar
1 tsp prepared mustard
1 small (5 oz) can tomato paste
½ tsp ground black pepper

CUT the herring into bite-size pieces. Mix all the other ingredients together. When doing this, however, first pour the sugar then the oil into a mixing bowl, mix slightly and add the rest (it won't blend so easily if you do it the other way around.)
PLACE a layer of herring, then a layer of the other ingredients, alternating, into a old-style glass canning jar with a rubber seal and a metal bale ("That's what bubbe did, so that's what I do!"). Use a knife to make sure the tomato sauce goes down all sides and covers the herring.
CLOSE the lid tightly and place in the refrigerator for 2 days. Serve cold.

Rubens family potato chremslach

Around the beautifully set table in Laila Rubens's welcoming apartment overlooking a leafy city park, the meaning of *The Jewish Kitchen* really came to life for me. Laila, Israeli-born but a long-term Antwerp resident, had organized, no, had truly orchestrated, a lunch – and what a lunch it was! – for which over a dozen women had each cooked a dish representative of their different Jewish backgrounds – Dutch, Siberian, Yemenite, Bukharan and many more. We all learned a lot that lunchtime, not least myself, and by the end everyone was enjoyably swopping and sharing recipes, many of which now appear in this book. My thanks go to Laila and all the women of Antwerp for a melting pot lunch that was simply unforgettable.

MAKES ABOUT 12
3 potatoes, peeled
salt and pepper
1–2 tbsp margarine, softened
3 egg whites
vegetable oil, for frying

BOIL the potatoes, drain and mash with the seasonings and margarine.
WHISK the egg whites until stiff and fold into the potatoes. The consistency should be quite soft.
HEAT some oil in a frying pan and when really hot, drop tablespoonfuls of the potato mixture into the pan and shallow-fry for a few minutes on each side until golden-brown on the outside and soft and fluffy inside. Drain on paper towel and serve right away.

Lithuanian pickled halibut

Henriette Kahn made this delicious cold fish dish for the communal Rosh Hashanah lunch that I attended in Trondheim. The recipe came from her mother-in-law Rosa, who was taught it by her own mother, Ida Ullmann, from Lithuania.

SERVES 6–8

⅞ cup white wine vinegar

1⅜ cups plus 1 tbsp sugar

1¾ cups water

1 large onion, thinly sliced

3–4 bay leaves

1 lemon, finely sliced

2 tbsp raisins

2 tbsp chopped almonds

1 tbsp ground ginger

salt

2 lb 4 oz halibut steaks

MAKE a brine with all the ingredients except the fish and boil gently for 20 minutes. Remove from the heat and add the halibut steaks.
COVER and leave for at least 30 minutes. When the fish is quite cold, place on a deep serving dish with the sauce and chill until needed. This is best made at least a day in advance.

Fish in Red Sea sauce

A popular Judeo-Spanish dish. The tomato sauce symbolizes the Red Sea crossed by the Israelites in their flight from Egypt.

SERVES 6

1 large onion, finely chopped

2–3 carrots, diced

2–3 celery stalks, diced

2–3 garlic cloves, finely chopped

5–6 tbsp olive oil

1 tsp sugar

2 x 14 oz cans tomatoes in tomato sauce (not juice)

paprika, to taste

juice of ½ lemon

salt and pepper

1 large bunch of parsley, finely chopped

1 lb 4 oz white fish fillets

SAUTÉ the onion, carrots, celery and garlic in the oil until soft.
ADD the sugar, tomatoes, paprika, some lemon juice and seasonings. Bring to a boil then simmer for about 20 minutes until thick.
STIR in the parsley and the rest of the lemon juice, then add the fish to the pan. Baste with the sauce and simmer for about 5–10 minutes.
REMOVE from the heat and let cool. Chill until needed, then serve at room temperature.

Italian tuna & rice salad

A popular summer Sabbath dish, usually made with canned tuna, but better still with fresh tuna.

SERVES 4–6

1 lb tuna steaks

olive oil, for brushing

salt

1¾ cups long-grain rice

14 oz jar artichokes in oil, drained and halved

6–8 anchovies in oil, drained and chopped

3½ oz black and/or green olives, pitted and chopped

2 tbsp capers

4 plum tomatoes, chopped

1–2 red onions, finely chopped

fresh basil and salad leaves (optional)

lemon wedges, to serve

DRESSING

6 tbsp extra virgin olive oil

1 tbsp Balsamic vinegar

1–2 garlic cloves, finely chopped

salt and pepper

MAKE the dressing by whisking the ingredients together. Set aside.
BRUSH the tuna steaks with olive oil, sprinkle with a little salt and grill for just 1½ minutes on each side, so the fish is just cooked, maybe still a little pink in the middle. Place on a board and cut into pieces, then toss in some dressing. Set aside.
COOK the rice according to the package instructions, drain and toss with the remaining dressing. Set aside to cool, then mix in the tuna and remaining ingredients, except the basil, salad leaves and lemon.
LET chill for a few hours. Just before serving, mix in some basil and salad leaves, if desired. Garnish with lemon wedges.

LEFT: ITALIAN TUNA & RICE SALAD

Spicy Libyan fish
Hraimeh

Ilana Yamin lives in a small bungalow on an Israeli *moshav* (agricultural settlement) along with other families who fled from Libya after 1954 when a savage pogrom in Tripoli killed more than 140 Jews. It marked the beginning of the end for this ancient Jewish community; from 38,000 strong in 1948, it fell to literally zero at the beginning of 2002 when Esmerelda Meghnagi, the last Jew in Libya, died.

A short, effervescent and highly religious lady, Ilana met us wearing a traditional white headdress, although she insisted on changing to her Sabbath hat for "formal" photographs. Her beaming moon-face shone with pleasure as she showed off her tiny kitchen and the array of seemingly endless pots and pans lined up on a hot plate with enough food to feed the Israeli army, or at least her husband and five children.

Her boundless energy and enthusiasm was a wonder to behold. Quite how she managed to fit in the time to cook, bake the challah breads, organize the boisterous household and work as a caregiver for elderly people was simply baffling. Although Ilana was born in Israel, both her parents are from Libya, she is married to a Libyan and most of her eight brothers and sisters are married to Libyans as well. Yamin, she said, meant "right" – as in the clenched right fist she jokingly held up to us, her cuddly, rotund frame shaking with laughter.

Every Friday she rises early to make dishes such as spicy soup with chicken; *mafroom* or potatoes stuffed with meat, served in a spicy red sauce; slow-cooked spicy meat casserole with beans and eggs; and fish in a spicy tomato sauce. In winter she makes a Sabbath stew with wheat berries and chard, as well as intestines stuffed with rice, liver, cilantro and spices. At Yom Kippur, the family break their fast on *sheket*, sweet almond milk, *boulo*, a rich bread sweetened with raisins and nuts, and *nukidas*, an Italian-influenced dish similar to gnocchi – their Italian heritage also shows in their fondness for spaghetti, but the sauce is always "much hotter than the Italians would have it."

Ilana sat down to discuss recipes, then immediately bounced up to fetch a plate of hand-made couscous with hand-peeled chickpeas and spicy vegetable sauce – laborious to make, she said with a big mock sigh, but the grains, she insisted, more delicate than other versions.

Up she jumped again to get a salad of chopped peppers, cucumbers, radish, carrots and pumpkin mashed with lemon and paprika.

The Jewish-Libyan kitchen without hot spice is like a fish without water. A homemade combination of hot paprika, mashed garlic and oil is the basis of almost every dish; you would never find a Libyan house without a jar of the fiery stuff in the fridge. Spread on bread and topped with canned tuna, it has become a favorite modern Libyan sandwich. To counteract the spiciness, they eat enamel-stripping quarters of lemon.

So, will her three daughters carry on her tradition of home cooking, I asked Ilana as she showered them with kisses while they tried to dodge past her on the way to watch TV? Maybe yes, maybe no, she shrugged expressively. Who knows? Only God knows. He knows everything.

Hraimeh has now become a popular Friday night dish throughout Israel. The amount of paprika used is a matter of personal taste, and Ilana makes it less spicy for her children.

SERVES 4
3 tbsp olive oil
⅜ cup plus 1 tbsp water
juice of 1 lemon
4–5 tbsp tomato paste
4 garlic cloves, finely chopped
pinch of salt
1 tsp ground cumin
½ tsp ground caraway seed
   (worth getting the pestle out
   for – the flavor makes a
   significant difference)

1–2 tsp fresh red chili, seeded
   and chopped, or a mix of hot
   and sweet paprika, to taste
4 tuna steaks
fresh cilantro or parsley,
   chopped, for serving
lemon wedges, to serve

MIX the oil, water, lemon juice, tomato paste, garlic, salt and spices.
POUR into a wide, shallow pan and simmer for 10 minutes.
ADD the fish, turning it over so it absorbs some sauce on both sides. Cover and cook over a low heat for 15 minutes. Sprinkle with fresh cilantro or parsley and serve with lemon wedges.

LEFT: FRESH SARDINES,
ESSAOUIRA, MOROCCO

Fresh sardines stuffed with herbs

A Moroccan-Jewish recipe from the excellent Lamalo Restaurant in Antwerp, Netherlands.

SERVES 2

12 fresh sardines, sliced (about 5 inches long)
1 oz fresh parsley, chopped
1½ oz fresh cilantro, chopped
½ tbsp rosemary, finely chopped
½ tbsp basil, finely chopped
2 cloves of garlic, finely chopped
1 tbsp sweet paprika
½ tsp cumin
⅜ cup olive oil
all-purpose flour, for coating
vegetable oil, for frying

ASK the fish market to gut the sardines and remove the head. With luck, they may also remove the backbone. If not, it is not hard to gently pull the spine away from the flesh with your fingers, rather like peeling off a Velcro strip. Flatten out each sardine, rinse well, pat dry and set aside.

COMBINE the herbs, garlic and spices with the olive oil. Place 1–2 tsp of this stuffing on top of a sardine fillet and cover, sandwich style, with another fillet. Press firmly together. Repeat with the other sardines.

LIGHTLY flour each side of the sardine sandwich.

SHALLOW-FRY the sardines in oil for several minutes on each side until they are crisp and brown.

SERVE with an arugula and tomato salad.

The Talmud says: "He who makes it a habit to eat small fish will not suffer from indigestion; even more, small fish make a man's whole body fruitful and virile."

Grilled trout Kinneret-style

This is the most popular way of cooking *musht* or St. Peter's fish (*Tilapia galilea*), unique to Lake Kinneret (aka the Sea of Galilee), although the fish is also served deep-fried or baked with tahini. Legend has it that the strangely thin body of the fish was the result of its biblical ancestors being cloven in two when the Israelites crossed the Red Sea in the Exodus from Egypt. St. Peter's fish also figures in a famous story that involves loaves and fishes, but that's for Another Kitchen.

SERVES 4
4 large fresh trout
2 garlic cloves
1 bunch parsley (or cilantro), chopped
1–2 preserved lemons, chopped
ground cumin, for rubbing
salt and pepper
juice of 1 lemon
extra virgin olive oil, for drizzling
lemon wedges, to serve

MAKE some diagonal slashes on both sides of each trout and insert thin slivers of garlic. Chop the rest of the garlic, mix with the parsley and preserved lemons and use to stuff the fish. Trout is already oily, so they should need no extra oil at this stage.

LIGHTLY rub the fish with a little cumin, seasonings and lemon juice. Turn tenderly, so the filling doesn't spill out and season the other side. Set aside to marinate for at least 15 minutes.

ARRANGE the fish on a large broiler rack covered with aluminum foil.

COOK the under a medium-hot broiler for about 6–7 minutes on one side, then 4–5 minutes on the other. The skin should start to become crisp and crackly, but if the fish seems to be drying out, sprinkle it with more lemon juice.

DRIZZLE with extra virgin olive oil, and serve with lemon wedges, plus salad and lots of *chippeles* (chips with a term of endearment).

Egyptian fish with lemon

SERVES 6–8
2 cloves garlic, finely chopped
4–5 tbsp olive oil
5 cups water
juice of 4–5 lemons
1 tsp turmeric
2 tsp salt
1½ oz fresh parsley, chopped
about 2 lb 4 oz fish steaks

LIGHTLY fry the garlic in the oil, then add the water, lemon juice, turmeric, salt and parsley. Bring to a boil and add the fish.

SIMMER gently for 30 minutes, then place the fish in a serving dish and cover with the cooking liquid. Let cool, then chill.

ABOVE: LAKE KINNERET, ISRAEL;
RIGHT: GRILLED TROUT KINNERET-STYLE

Anglo-Jewish gefilte fish

In Eastern Europe, gefilte fish was originally the poached forcemeat made from carp or pike, stuffed back into the skin and served cold on the Sabbath, thus avoiding the need to separate bones from the fish, which is viewed as a form of work. Nowadays the term refers to the chopped forcemeat alone, made into balls and either fried or poached in fish stock and topped with a slice of carrot like a little orange-gold *yarmulke* (skullcap). For chopped and boiled fish, use plenty of bones and fish heads so the stock turns to jelly when cold.

My late mother based her method on that of the legendary Florence Greenberg who started her cooking column in the *Jewish Chronicle* in 1920. Mrs. G. included chopped parsley, but I think it spoils the pure look of the fish. As to the question of sugar in the mix, well, I go with the Litvak side of the family and avoid it. The Polish tradition includes sugar, historically linked to the growth of the sugar beet industry in the 19th century. But, then, there's no accounting for taste.

SERVES 4–6

2 lb 4 oz white fish, skinned and boned (I prefer a three-way mix of hake, haddock and cod – hake, in my opinion, is essential for delicacy of flavor)
1 large onion
1 tbsp ground almonds
2 eggs, beaten
salt and white pepper
medium matzo meal

FISH STOCK

head, skin and bones of non-oily fish (remember more bones, more jelly!)
1 quart water
1 onion, sliced
1 celery stick
2 large carrots, sliced

Ball and Chraine

The distinguished Israeli chef Reuven Harel made the *Guinness Book of Records* in 2002 with the largest gefilte fish ball in the world. His recipe included 660 pounds carp, 450 eggs, 35 pounds onions and weighed in at a ball-breaking 330 pounds. When I met him, he told me he was planning the largest kugel, kubba and challah (65 feet long) for 2003. "Why not another gefilte fish attempt?" I asked. "No, once is enough," he replied, "you've got to keep moving on."

FOR CHOPPED AND FRIED:

BRING the ingredients for the stock to a boil in the measured water, then simmer for a good 30 minutes. Strain and reserve the liquid.

COARSELY mince the fish with the onion and mix with the almonds, eggs and seasoning.

ADD enough matzo meal to make the mixture fairly stiff. Wet your hands and roll into balls about 3 inches in diameter.

SHALLOW-FRY in 1 inch of oil, flattening them slightly, until they are golden-brown on both sides.

DRAIN on paper towel and serve cold with *chrane* (beet and horseradish sauce).

FOR CHOPPED AND BOILED:

MAKE the stock as above.

MINCE the fish as above and shape into balls.

POACH gently, covered, in the fish stock for 1 hour.

TRANSFER the fish balls carefully onto a serving dish. Spoon over some stock and top each fish ball with a slice of carrot. Chill until cold, and serve with *chrane*.

LEFT: FISH FROM THE
GALILEE, ISRAEL; RIGHT:
ESSAOUIRA, MOROCCO

Dutch fish cakes

Viskoekjes

The recipe for these simple little fish-cakes comes from Vera Drilzma of Antwerp. They are much loved by Dutch Jews, who often break their fast on them after Yom Kippur.

SERVES 6

1 onion, finely chopped

¼ cup margarine or butter, plus extra for frying

2 lb 4 oz cod, cooked and flaked

2 eggs

1 lb 4 oz potatoes, boiled and mashed

1 oz parsley, chopped

pinch of nutmeg or mace

salt and pepper

matzo meal or dried breadcrumbs, for coating

vegetable oil, for frying

GENTLY fry the onion in the margarine or butter and let cool.

MIX with the rest of the ingredients and chill until firm. If the mixture seems too thick, add a little water or milk to moisten.

MAKE small cakes and coat with matzo meal or dried breadcrumbs. (If desired, set aside in the refrigerator, at this point, until needed.)

SHALLOW-FRY in oil for 3–4 minutes on both sides until brown. Drain on paper towel and serve right away.

Moroccan fish boulettes

MAKES ABOUT 30

(SERVES 4 AS A MAIN COURSE)

1 lb ground white fish (either a single variety or mixed)

pinch of saffron threads, soaked in a little hot water

rind of 1 lemon

salt and pepper

1 egg, beaten

1 tbsp chopped parsley or cilantro

⅔ cup medium matzo meal

SAUCE

5 tbsp water

3 tbsp olive oil

1 onion, grated

1 garlic clove, crushed

½ tsp paprika

½ tsp ground cumin

pinch of cayenne or red pepper flakes

3 large tomatoes, skinned, seeded and chopped

juice of ½ lemon

PUT all the ingredients for the sauce in a shallow pan wide enough to hold the fish balls in one layer. Bring to a boil and simmer for 10–15 minutes.

MIX all the ingredients for the fish boulettes together and form small balls, the size of walnuts.

GENTLY add them to the sauce and poach for 15 minutes, carefully turning halfway through. Serve with rice or couscous.

In Genesis, God instructs both fish and man to "be fruitful and multiply." As a result, the "day of the fish" became a symbolic ritual in some Sephardi communities, when a new bride would step three times over a tray of fish, to wish for fertility in the marriage.

Moroccan fish with chickpeas and cilantro

Aliza Sadan-Shir's parents both came to Israel from Fez, Morocco, in 1947; Aliza's taxi-driver husband Rafi came the same year, at age two. They now live in Holon, south of Tel Aviv, in a top floor, open concept design apartment, smartly furnished with aqua leather sofas, glass tables and elaborate chandeliers, and with a doorway decorated with pictures of Moroccan sages and holy amulets. Every Friday morning Aliza makes an early start, cooking a great array of dishes in preparation for the Sabbath.

Aliza is a naturally gifted cook who, despite the demands of her own working life, would rather die than go and purchase any of the great array of ready-made Moroccan foods on sale in every Israeli supermarket. Largely self-taught, she only cooks the food her family enjoys most. "Whenever I try and do something different, my husband says, please don't bother! We like subtle flavors to the food, in fact it is only my Ashkenazi son-in-law who likes his food really spicy."

The Friday I came she was making a typical selection of dishes: beef braised with onions, mushrooms, turmeric and white pepper; roasted peppers with garlic and lemon; roasted eggplant and tomatoes with green chili peppers, scallions and lemon; carrots with paprika, cumin, lemon and garlic; chard with garlic, cumin, paprika and garlic; beets with garlic, lemon and parsley; chicken with potatoes, paprika and turmeric; and fish with chickpeas, red pepper and cilantro, a particular favorite in Moroccan homes on Friday nights. The dishes that would appear on the table later that evening would number at least twice as many.

Aliza was dictating recipes as fast as I could write: artichoke hearts stuffed with ground beef with peas and celeriac; pumpkin and carrot couscous; sardines stuffed with cilantro, garlic, cumin and paprika. Like a slot machine delivering the jackpot, they kept on coming… and coming, but we were running short of time, Sabbath was approaching, the table had to be set with the (homemade) challah and wine. The aromas wafting from the stove were mouthwatering. I said her husband was a lucky man to have such a talented cook as a wife. Aliza only smiled and kept on cooking.

Aliza makes this with thick fillets of Nile perch, but other white fish such as cod, haddock, pollock or red drum can be substituted. I have also slightly adapted her original recipe in a way more suited to my own Mancunian-Jewish Kitchen.

SERVES 4

4 white fish fillets, about 6 oz each

salt

juice of 1 lemon

2 tbsp extra virgin olive oil, plus some extra to finish

3 garlic cloves, crushed

2 red peppers, seeded and cut into strips

1 tbsp sweet paprika

2 tsp of cumin

¼ tsp turmeric

generous pinch of red pepper flakes

1 cup chickpeas, soaked overnight and drained

4–5 tomatoes (or a 15 oz can), skinned, seeded and chopped

large bunch of fresh cilantro, chopped

salt and white pepper, to taste

1 fresh lemon or preserved lemon, cut into chunks

SPRINKLE the fish with salt and some of the lemon juice and let marinate for 30 minutes – this firms up the flesh and sweetens the flavor. Rinse the fish and set aside.

HEAT the oil in a wide, shallow casserole dish, add the garlic and cook gently until the aroma rises up.

ADD the red peppers, paprika, cumin, turmeric and red pepper flakes and cook for a few more minutes.

ADD the chickpeas and enough water to cover (if using canned tomatoes add them now). Bring to a boil, then cover and simmer for about 40–45 minutes until the chickpeas are cooked. If using fresh tomatoes, add them now along with two-thirds of the cilantro. Season to taste.

LAY the fish fillets on top and finish with the remaining lemon juice, cilantro, the fresh or preserved lemon chunks – plus a good slug of extra virgin olive oil.

COVER and simmer gently for 10–15 minutes until the fish is cooked.

This can also be served at room temperature or made the day before and reheated.

Berlin: *Kaffee und Kuchen*

MRS. SOPHIE STEINER'S POPPY SEED CAKE HAS HAD A LONG JOURNEY. A RECIPE, YOU COULD SAY, OF MANY PASSPORTS, AS WELL AS MEMORIES, IT HAS TRAVELED FROM POLAND TO FRANKFURT, VIENNA, STRASBOURG AND ISRAEL – ALWAYS A SMALL, SWEET TASTE OF HOME.

And, now, it has metaphorically returned full-circle to Germany, where it is regularly baked by her daughter, Gaby Nonhoff, a professional caterer in Berlin.

I met them both at the Cafe Oren next to the Neue Synagoge, its gilded onion dome a landmark since 1866. Sophie recalled the food of her German-Jewish childhood: the six-stranded challah bread baked by her mother, the gefilte fish and homemade lokshen with chicken soup on Fridays. "Mother would make exceptionally fine noodles, but it was such a performance. Every surface in the house would be covered with drying pasta. Usually we had *braten* (slow-cooked pot roast) and potato kugel, but when there were guests we ate goose with sauerkraut and potato dumplings. It was so good! In winter my mother would preserve goose liver in its fat to be eaten at Pesach. And every Thursday, she would bake three kinds of cake to eat for breakfast on Shabbat."

The tradition of *Kaffee und Kuchen* between 4 and 5 p.m. was transported to the cafes of Tel Aviv, a city much influenced by German-Jewish Bauhaus architecture and innovative musical and literary expression. One reason, perhaps, why many Israelis find an affinity with the city, as well as the wave of creative energy arising from this freshly-minted, new euro-capital of glittering glass and brick.

Challenging architectural concepts, provocative street installations and monumental new cityscapes re-occupy the old, ideological battlegrounds. Gangling cranes fill the skyline like rainbow dinosaurs. Playful statues of Berliner bears, the city's symbol, captivate not intimidate. The no-man's land of Potsdamer Platz has been transformed into a soaring mega-mall; the Reichstag reinvented with its futuristic Norman Foster dome; and the startling British embassy is a symbolic statement about the collapse of the wall. Hermès has opened a shop within sight of the old Stasi offices, and there are "chicky-micky" bagel bars and falafel stands, modern icons of Jewish life if not classic German-Jewish food, on many a newly restored street corner.

Berlin mingles celluloid glamor with kitsch domesticity, sleaze with performance art. Here, the strands of modern European history flicker past like spools of newsreel film. Jewish Berlin, past and present, also takes its place. The many memorials that dot this complicated city are testament to a presence that dates back over 700 years, and to a huge community whose merchants, bankers, scientists, writers, artists and philosophers helped power Berlin into a leading world capital.

This necessary confrontation of the past has brought reconciliation and historical self-awareness – too much for some, never enough for others. There are the showpiece memorials: the silver-zinc lightning-flash cum broken Star of David of Daniel Libeskind's powerful Jewish Museum, a human void in concrete form; the controversial Holocaust Memorial that will be a field of stone stela.

"The strands of modern European history flicker past like spools of newsreel film."

CLOCKWISE FROM TOP CENTER:
THE REICHSTAG DOME;
THE REICHTSTAG INTERIOR;
A BERLIN BEAR;
THE NEUE SYNAGOGE;
THE JEWISH MUSEUM

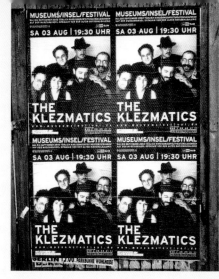

FAR LEFT: KLEZMER CONCERT
POSTERS; LEFT: PART OF THE
BERLIN WALL

Then there are the smaller memorials: a set of mirrors in the former garment district remembers Jews from the textile trade; a subterranean sculpture of an empty library is dedicated to the 1933 book-burning; small signs, mute statements of the Nazi anti-Jewish laws, hang from the lampposts of an ordinary residential district.

In the Jewish restaurants, especially in the old Jewish Quarter in a revitalized part of East Berlin, the majority of customers are, ironically, non-Jewish. The fashion for gefilte fish and klezmer music reflects a welcome interest in things Jewish, but the whim of tourism is perhaps a less solid basis for the future than that of genuine community demand. The argument is that such expressions of Jewish culture are hollow without their spiritual dimension. Which comes first, however, in such a brutally devastated community, is as difficult as any chicken (soup) and egg conundrum. Many of the big issues of Jewish life, in particular how Judaism relates to the modern world, first emerged in Berlin – the ongoing debates are part of a long tradition.

The official Jewish community currently registers around 12,000 affiliated members plus more "under the radar." That there are Jews here at all may still surprise, but the belief that a Germany without Jews would be the ultimate triumph for Hitler is one to which many subscribe. Others are here simply because of marriage or work, others are descendants of post-war displaced persons, and there is also a number of original *yekkes*, German Jews, who survived the camps or emerged from hiding and chose to stay or were unable to settle elsewhere. A few returned to build a new Germany in the East.

The great majority, however, are from the former Soviet Union, recent refugees from anti-semitism, encouraged by German economic and welfare assistance – a fact of realpolitik that subverts the oft quoted claim that the city has the fastest growing Jewish population in the world. Many have no knowledge of Jewish religious life or ritual; often only a trace memory remains of grandmothers lighting Sabbath candles – or a family recipe. The great wave of diverse Soviet immigrants, from Ukrainians to Georgians, has in many ways reinvigorated the community but has also brought difficulties: the new arrivals have been accused of opportunism, while the host establishment has been described as inflexible. Inevitable, perhaps, in a city where the ordinary is still extraordinary and where much healing remains to be done.

The existential state of Jewish Berlin may be a work in progress, but Galina Grodynskaya, for one, is thoroughly at ease with her new identity as a modern Jewish Berliner. She came from Moscow in 1990 and works at the Jewish Community Center, but she has not forgotten the past. "We were pretty assimilated, only going to the synagogue on high holidays," she recalled, "but we never ate pork and did have matzo at Passover. Luckily my grandmother, who had lived in a Hassidic *shtetl* near Kiev, remembered the old recipes – she stuffed the whole carp to make gefilte fish; I do it the lazy way, poaching balls of minced fish. And you have to add a little sugar to take away any muddy taste – that's what she always used to say. I also add a bit of sugar to chicken soup, but now I mostly cook vegetarian!

"On Fridays, we would have a chicken and sometimes my grandmother would make stuffed chicken neck or knishes. She also made a dark honey cake with buckwheat honey, raisins and walnuts. Another of her specialities was matzo meal kugel – she made it in a huge, heavy casserole that she brought with her from Russia. You can cook anything in it, and it never burns. Although she died a few years ago, I still use it because it reminds me of her. Whatever she made was so delicious, she managed to turn everything into a feast!"

Sophie's poppy seed torte
Mohnkuchen

Poppy seeds are popular in Jewish cooking because they are symbolic of the blessing of the manna in the desert. At Purim, they are also eaten in memory of Queen Esther, who is said to have fasted for three days, subsisting on seeds alone, before approaching Ahasuerus to plead for the life of her people.

You can grind the poppy seeds in a clean coffee grinder, but the recipe also works perfectly well if the seeds are left whole.

6 eggs, separated
1 cup sugar
1 cup poppy seeds, ground
½ cup chopped walnuts
⅓ cup raisins

TOPPING
7 tbsp margarine or butter
3½ oz baking chocolate unsweetened, broken into pieces
2 tbsp water

PREHEAT the oven to 350°F.

GREASE and line a 10½-inch springform cake pan.

WHISK the egg whites with a pinch of salt until they form snowy peaks, then slowly whisk in half the sugar. When the mixture is really stiff, chill until needed.

BEAT the egg yolks and remaining sugar until creamy and light yellow. Add 4 tablespoons of the chocolate topping and mix well.

STIR the poppy seeds, walnuts and raisins into the egg-chocolate mix.

FOLD half of the egg whites into the poppy seed mixture, then stir in the remainder and pour into the cake pan

BAKE for 40–45 minutes or until a skewer inserted in the center of the cake comes out clean.

LET cool in the pan. Gently loosen the sides with a knife and remove from the pan.

MELT the margarine or butter for the topping, take off the heat, add the chocolate and water and stir until melted. Pour over the cake and let cool before serving.

FAR LEFT: JEWISH QUARTER,
PARIS; LEFT: KOSHER WINE

THREE CAKES FOR PASSOVER

Almond cake

This moist-textured cake is best the day after it is made. Serve with whipped cream or fruit, perhaps a berry compote.

5 egg whites (at room temperature)
pinch of salt
½ cup superfine granulated sugar
1⅔ cups ground almonds
grated zest of 1 orange
1 tbsp orange liqueur (optional)
¼ cup slivered almonds

PREHEAT the oven to 375°F.

GREASE and line an 8-inch springform cake pan.

WHISK the egg whites with the salt until they stand in soft peaks. Whisking constantly, add the sugar a little at a time. Continue whisking until the mixture is firm, shiny and very thick.

FOLD in the ground almonds, orange zest and liqueur (if using) with a metal spoon. Pour the mixture into the cake pan and sprinkle the slivered almonds over the top.

BAKE for 30 minutes or until a skewer inserted into the center comes out clean.

ALLOW to stand in the pan for 10 minutes, then loosen, turn out and let cool on a wire rack.

Carrot cake from Aargau

This old recipe comes from Swiss food writer Käthi Frenkel-Bloch. She explains that, until 1866, Jews were restricted to two villages in the canton of Aargau, and thus their culinary traditions were constrained by the availability of regional and seasonal ingredients. Chicken was the main ingredient of the Sabbath meal, along with beans and root vegetables, but they were rarely able, for example, to make gefilte fish because the village streams were too small to sustain carp ponds. At Pesach, in addition to matzo recipes, many dishes relied on old potatoes: kugel, salad, soup and so on and on. Carrot cake became popular, simply because carrots were cheap and available year-round. This is Käthi's Pesach version.

1 cup superfine granulated
    sugar
7 oz carrots, peeled and finely
    grated
1⅞ cups ground almonds
5 eggs, separated

grated zest and juice of
    1 lemon or 1–2 tbsp Kirsch
1 heaping tbsp fine or cake
    matzo meal
2 tsp baking powder
potato flour, for dusting

PREHEAT the oven to 350°F.

MIX the egg yolks and sugar until foamy.

ADD the carrots, almonds, lemon zest and juice or Kirsch, matzo meal and baking powder.

GREASE a 9½-inch springform cake pan and dust with potato flour.

WHISK the egg whites until stiff and fold into the cake mixture. Pour the mixture into the pan and bake for about 45 minutes. Test by lightly touching the surface of the cake – it should feel dryish and soft, rather like cotton wool, but not hard.

ALLOW to stand in the pan for 10 minutes, then loosen from the pan, turn out and let cool on a wire rack.

(Note: This cake is best left uncut for several days, to allow the flavors to mature. It can also be covered with white frosting or fondant icing and decorated with marzipan carrots.)

Sponge cake

Pesach wouldn't be Pesach without a sponge cake, whether it is the *plava* of Eastern Europe or Sephardi *pan d'Espagna*. Passover sponges are usually made with a combination of cake flour and potato flour, but this version, which uses just the latter, gives a particularly creamy and fragile texture. The sponge cake repertoire depends on laborious whisking to keep them light and airy – another reason to give thanks at the Festival of Freedom for the liberation of the food mixer.

6 eggs, separated
1 cup superfine granulated
    sugar
3 tbsp lemon juice
3 tbsp orange juice

2 tbsp orange zest
2 tbsp lemon zest
pinch of salt
⅞ cup potato flour, sifted
    several times

PREHEAT the oven to 300°F.

GREASE an 8-inch square or round nonstick cake pan and dust lightly with potato flour.

WHISK the egg yolks and sugar for about 5 minutes until pale and creamy, then add the juice and zest. Continue to beat for another 10 minutes until the batter thickens, and expands in bulk, even further.

WHISK the egg whites and salt in a separate bowl, until just firm and glossy, but take care not to overbeat. Lightly fold them into the cake mixture, then gradually sprinkle in the potato flour, folding in carefully after each addition.

POUR the thick, foamy batter into the cake pan and tap it sharply on the countertop to burst any air bubbles. Bake immediately for 1 hour 10 minutes until the sponge is well risen, comes away from the side of the pan and is lightly colored.

LEAVE in the pan on a wire rack until completely cold. The cake will fall slightly as it cools.

REMOVE carefully from the pan and serve.

Easy apple strudel

You can use phyllo pastry but ready-made puff pastry is easier, faster, less fragile and tastes just as good. Different, but still good. Let's face it, nothing will taste quite like the real thing, for which you need a large table, huge white cloth, arms like baseball bats with which to flail the dough then stretch it until paper-thin, an army of helpers, the patience of a saint, etc, etc. Dream on, this is the 21st century.

SERVES 4–6

1 package (13 oz)ready-made
   and rolled puff pastry
apricot jam
1 lb Granny Smith apples,
   peeled, sliced and tossed
   in lemon juice
2 tbsp golden raisins, soaked in
   2 tbsp Calvados or Amaretto

2 tbsp toasted sliced or
   chopped almonds
2 tbsp brown sugar
2 tsp apple pie spice
margarine or butter
1 egg white, whisked with
   1 tbsp water

PREHEAT the oven to 350°F.

SCHMEAR the pastry with apricot jam.

MIX the apples, golden raisins, almonds, sugar and apple pie spice and make an off-center, log-shaped filling parallel to the wider side of the pastry rectangle. Dot with a little margarine or butter, then roll up the pastry and tuck in the sides to keep the filling from escaping. Place on a baking sheet with the seam on the underside.

BRUSH with the egg white and bake for about 40 minutes. Let stand for at least 15 minutes before gently cutting into portions – this can be tricky as bits of pastry invariably make a bid for freedom, but most of the strudel should hold together.

SERVE either warm or at room temperature.

Tu B'Shevat dried fruit filling

⅜ cup plus 1 tbsp brown sugar
⅞ cup shredded coconut
⅓ cup raisins
⅔ cup sliced almonds
⅓ cup chopped dates

⅓ cup dried cherries
⅓ cup chopped figs
2 tbsp ground almonds
zest of 1 orange
zest of 1 lemon

MIX well together and sprinkle over the pastry, leaving a 1-inch margin around the edges. Dot with a little margarine or butter, roll up, brush with egg white and bake for 40 minutes.

Zena's lekach
Honey cake

My friend Zena Swerling first started cooking many years ago, when she was just tall enough to get her chin "over mummy's kitchen table." As she says, this is one of those cakes that never comes out quite the same each time you make it, but always tastes good!

Zena says you can use any glass you like – as long as you use the same one for all the measurements, but the one she normally uses holds 8 fl oz.

MAKES 2 CAKES: A 2 lb CAKE AND A 1 lb CAKE

1 glass sugar ("sugar sugar –
   in the old days, who knew
   from different sugars?")
1 glass water
1 glass vegetable oil
cup honey or molasses or any
   combination you please
   ("i.e., anything that's in the
   store cupboard that you
   want to use up")

3 medium eggs
1 tsp baking soda
ground ginger, to taste (try
   1 well-rounded tsp)
½ tsp apple pie spice
all-purpose flour, as needed
walnuts or thinly sliced apple
   (optional)

PREHEAT the oven to 350°F.

GREASE and line with parchment paper a 1 lb and a 2 lb loaf pan.

MIX all the ingredients together, with sufficient flour to make a thin batter – "like pouring cream."

POUR into the loaf pans and top, if desired, with walnuts or apple slices.

BAKE for about 1¼ hours respectively. The top should feel firm and spring back when pressed gently.

REMOVE from the oven, leave in the pan for 5 minutes then turn onto a wire rack to cool. Wrap tightly in aluminum foil and leave to mature for a few days before serving.

RIGHT: ZENA'S LEKACH

Linzertorte

This recipe came with a warning. Freya Maier, age 92, still lives in the Bronx, but she was born in Kippenheim, a small village with 200 Jews in the Black Forest region of Germany. During the war, Freya and her husband Ludwig booked a passage to New World freedom on the ill-fated *Saint Louis*, which was cruelly prevented from docking in Havana, Cuba. The Maiers were subsequently among the lucky ones who spent six months interned in southern England before being allowed to leave for New York; most of the other passengers perished back in Europe. According to her niece, Fay Wertheimer, Linzertorte is Freya's trademark; and until a recent accident, she was "in regular LT production!"

Freya's daughter Sonja, however, could only supply a rough outline of this legendary family recipe, stressing that no one in the family could bake it as well as her mother, and warning against including it in the book for that reason.

Well, there's nothing like a challenge – and while I am quite sure this ersatz version does not match up to Freya's original, it still produces an excellent cake for those who, sadly, know no better.

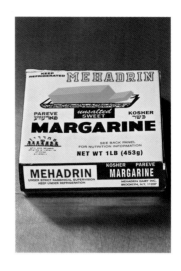

SERVES 8–10

1¾ cups shelled whole hazelnuts

7 oz baking chocolate unsweetened

⅞ cup cake matzo meal (or use half meal and half all-purpose flour)

1 cup superfine granulated sugar

1–2 tsp ground cinnamon

generous pinch of ground cloves

⅞ cup margarine (or butter)

3 eggs, gently whisked

1 tbsp Cognac or brandy

1 tbsp very strong coffee (cold, of course)

1–2 12 oz jars good quality raspberry jam

1–2 cups fresh raspberries (optional)

confectioners' sugar, for dusting

PREHEAT the oven to 350°F.

TOAST the hazelnuts in the oven until golden (watch like a hawk, one minute they are pale, the next a burned offering). When cool, grind in a food processor until the texture is similar but not quite as fine as ground almonds.

MELT the chocolate slowly in a bowl over a pan of hot water, then set aside to cool.

ADD the matzo meal, sugar, spices and margarine to the processor and grind briefly, but do not overprocess.

ADD the chocolate, eggs, brandy and coffee, and grind again until well mixed, softish and sticky. Press two-thirds of the mixture into a 10-inch flan pan with a removable bottom.

MAKE sure there are no gaps, then fill with raspberry jam.

USE some of the reserved pastry mix to make a lip around the top edge of the pastry shell to prevent the contents from bubbling over during baking.

MAKE a traditional lattice pattern with the remaining pastry, if desired.

PLACE on a baking sheet and bake for 30–35 minutes. When cool, carefully remove from the pan. Dust with confectioners' sugar and pile with fresh raspberries, if desired. (Serve with tiny cups of strong coffee).

FAR LEFT AND LEFT: JEWISH
BAKERY IN MANCHESTER,
ENGLAND

Chocolate babka

A recipe from British-born Leonie Birnbaum of Antwerp. Gooey and sticky. Like all Jewish cooks, however, I can't resist a little meddling, and although she doesn't include it in her recipe, some grated orange zest in the filling would make this *babka* (literally "little grandmother's bread") even more irresistible.

MAKES A 12- TO 16-INCH ROLL
4¼ cups all-purpose flour
1 cup plus 2 tbsp warm water
¾ oz active dried yeast,
   reconstituted in half the
   water or 1½ oz fresh yeast
½ cup vegetable oil
⅔ cup sugar

TOPPING
3 tbsp baking cocoa powder
1 cup plus 2 tbsp hot chocolate
   mix
3 tbsp sugar
8 tbsp raisins
1–2 tbsp vegetable oil

MIX the flour, yeast, remaining water, oil and sugar. Knead well, cover with a clean dish towel and let stand in a warm place for 1–2 hours until well risen.
PREHEAT the oven to 350°F.
GREASE a baking sheet or line with parchment paper.
MIX the cocoa powder, hot chocolate mix, sugar and raisins.
PUNCH down the dough and knead again. Roll out into a square about 12 to 16 inches wide. Cover with the cocoa mixture and sprinkle with a little oil. Roll up like a Swiss roll (you can bring the ends together to make a ring, if you like) and bake for 45 minutes. The bottom of the cake should sound hollow when tapped. Let stand 5 minutes on the baking sheet, then turn onto a wire rack to cool.

A Heavenly Babka

The Yiddish author Peretz wrote about a saintly character called Bontshe the Silent who quietly suffered all his life in poverty. When he finally arrived in heaven, he was honored by the angels for his noble and good character and was allowed to choose one object of his heart's desire. With trembling joy, he replied: "A babka, still warm, yes – and even with butter on it!"

Sfenz
Libyan Hanukkah doughnuts

Doughnuts, in one form or another, are traditional at Hanukkah throughout the Jewish world, as the sweet, deep-fried pastries are said to resemble the cakes eaten by the Maccabees. In Israel, every baker makes *soufganiyot*, or jam-filled doughnuts, but other versions, such as Tunisian *yoyos*, Greek *loukomades*, Persian *zelebi* or these Libyan *sfenz* are dipped in syrup after deep-frying.

MAKES ABOUT 12

2 eggs, beaten

¼ cup sugar

2 tbsp vegetable oil

1 tsp baking powder

1 cup plus 2 tbsp all-purpose flour

zest of 1 orange

⅔ cup finely chopped almonds

½ tsp orangeflower water

vegetable oil, for deep-frying

SYRUP

⅜ cup orange blossom honey

¼ cup water

1 tsp lemon juice

½ tsp orangeflower water

few drops of vanilla extract

MIX the ingredients for the syrup in a pan and heat gently, stirring occasionally, until the honey is dissolved.

BRING to a boil, but avoid stirring until the syrup has thickened. This should take about 30 minutes, then keep on a low heat until needed.

MIX all the ingredients for the doughnuts, adding a little more flour if necessary to make a firm dough. Knead for a few minutes until smooth.

ROLL out the dough and stamp circles with a 3-inch round pastry cutter. Use a smaller pastry cutter or glass to form the inner hole of the doughnut.

HEAT a pan half-filled with oil to 350°F and deep-fry a few doughnuts at a time (they will puff up so don't overcrowd the pan). When they are brown on both sides, remove and drain on paper towels, then place on a wire cooling rack set over a plate or on more paper towels.

REMOVE the syrup from the heat and spoon over both sides of the still-warm doughnuts, turning them with a fork or tongs.

SERVE immediately.

Orecchi di Aman
Haman's ears

As a modern cyber-commentary on Jewish festivals neatly puts it: "They tried to kill us, we won, let's eat!" And, it's an injunction that is particularly true at Purim, when pastries and fritters symbolizing parts of the body or clothing of the wicked Haman are consumed as a way of mocking and erasing the name of this ancient enemy. Triangular *hamantaschen* (representing pockets or a three-cornered hat) are the most popular in Eastern European communities, but Sephardi Jews prefer deep-fried, twisted "Haman's ears." The idea for using seeds and candied peel in this Italian version comes from *Le Ricette di Casa Mia* by Milka Belgrado Passigli.

MAKES ABOUT 36

1 cup all-purpose flour, sifted with ½ tsp baking power and a pinch of salt

1 egg, lightly beaten

1 tbsp olive oil

2 tbsp orangeflower water

2 tbsp superfine granulated sugar

1 tbsp fennel seeds

1 cup chopped candied peel

vegetable oil, for deep-frying

confectioners' sugar, for dusting

MIX the flour with the egg, olive oil, orangeflower water, sugar, fennel seeds and candied peel to make a soft dough. Turn on to a floured surface and knead well until smooth. Cover with plastic wrap and chill for at least 1 hour.

ROLL out as thinly as possible and cut into diamonds (about 4 inches in diameter) or ribbon shapes (about 5 x 1 inch). Slightly twist or pinch each one in the middle.

ALTERNATIVELY, pinch off small balls and shape and twist by hand. The shapes do not have to be perfect – Haman's ears were said to be pointed and irregular.

DEEP-FRY one or two at a time briefly in hot oil (375°F) on each side until puffy and light brown. Keep an eye on the temperature of the oil, as they can easily burn.

DRAIN on paper towel and sprinkle with confectioners' sugar when cool. Either eat right away or store in an airtight container.

Frou-frou chalet

This recipe for the eve of Yom Kippur is based on one from Madame Huguette Uhry de Bollwiller, and is courtesy of the Jewish Alsace website (www.sdv.fr/judaisme). *Chalet* or *schalet*, which derives from the Old French word for "warm," is historically linked to the Sabbath *cholent*. It is also related to the pudding now known as apple charlotte – although, in this case, without the bread casing. Quite where the frou-frou part comes from, I've not yet established – but I love the name, and the delicious, light pudding is good enough to enjoy with or without the subsequent fast.

8 eggs, separated
1¼ cups sugar
2 tbsp Kirsch
4 tbsp all-purpose flour

⅔ cup chopped almonds
4 apples, peeled, cored and
  finely sliced

PREHEAT the oven to 350°F.
CREAM the egg yolks with the sugar, add the Kirsch and mix well.
SIFT in the flour and almonds, then the apples.
BEAT the egg whites until firm and snowy, then gradually fold them into the pudding.
LIGHTLY grease a baking dish approximately 8 x 12 x ¾ inch. Pour in the cake mixture and bake for at least 1 hour until the sponge top is firm and golden.

Pineapple fritters à la Célestine

Israeli food and wine writer Daniel Rogov included this 19th century recipe in his column for the *Ha'aretz* newspaper. Between 1850 and 1878, Célestine Benditte-Strauss, the daughter of the Chief Rabbi of Lyon, was also the owner of the city's prestigious and fashionable Restaurant Cercle. As Rogov says, "What most of her clients never realized was that, because their hostess adhered to the laws of kashrut, she never tasted any of the dishes that were prepared at her restaurant. She did, however, have a passion for pineapple… Roger Veldam, the chef at the Cercle, dedicated several dishes to her, and this recipe has become a Hanukkah classic among Jewish families in Lyon."

SERVES 6–8
2 large pineapples, peeled,
  cored and thickly sliced
superfine granulated sugar, for
  dredging
¼ cup Kirsch
3 cups all-purpose flour
1 cup warm water
⅞ cup beer

1 tbsp vegetable oil
1 tbsp brandy
pinch of salt
2 egg whites, whisked
apricot jam, for spreading
vegetable oil, for deep-frying
superfine granulated sugar, for
  sprinkling

DREDGE the pineapple with sugar, then sprinkle generously with the Kirsch. Let steep for 30–40 minutes.
SIFT the flour and mix with the water, beer, oil, brandy and salt to make a batter.
DRY the pineapple slices on paper towel, then coat them with a thin layer of apricot jam.
WHILE the oil is heating, fold the whisked egg whites into the batter.
TAKE the fruit and batter to the stove. When the oil is hot (350°F), dip the pineapple slices into the batter, then fry until golden brown on both sides.
SERVE hot, sprinkled with sugar, if desired.

RIGHT: PINEAPPLE FRITTERS A LA CELESTINE

Old-fashioned sweet carrot kugel
Carrot Pudding

Carrots are much eaten at Rosh Hashanah because of their color, which symbolizes prosperity, and also because the Yiddish word for carrot is *mern*, which also means "to increase." Therefore, we eat carrots in hopes of a prosperous individual and communal year ahead. This kugel is also made at Pesach.

SERVES 4–6

3 tbsp potato flour
8 tbsp sweet red or fortified wine
1 lb carrots, grated
⅜ cup plus 1 tbsp brown sugar
8 tbsp fine matzo meal
1 tsp baking powder
1 tsp ground cinnamon
zest of 1 lemon
juice of 1 lemon
1 egg, beaten
⅓ cup raisins
⅓ cup chopped dates
pinch of salt
7 tbsp margarine (or butter), melted

PREHEAT the oven to 350°F.

DISSOLVE the potato flour in the wine, then mix with the remaining ingredients and combine well.

SPOON the mixture into a greased, shallow 8x10-inch baking pan and bake for 1 hour until crusty and amber in color.

SERVE hot, eat in good health and go to sleep for the rest of the afternoon.

Lokshen kugel
Noodle pudding

Rabbi Pinchas of Koritz was said to have observed that lokshen is eaten on the Sabbath because noodles, symbolic of Jewish unity, are so entangled they can never be separated.

SERVES 4–6

8 oz fine egg noodles (or medium, according to preference)
⅜ cup margarine (or butter)
¼ cup sugar
3 eggs, separated
⅜ cup plus 1 tbsp orange juice
1 cup raisins
1 cup chopped almonds
½ cup candied peel
½ tsp ground ginger
1 tsp cinnamon

PREHEAT the oven to 400°F.

GREASE a baking dish, about 8 x 10 inches.

COOK the noodles according to the package instructions, drain and place in the baking dish.

CREAM the margarine and sugar until light. Beat in the egg yolks one by one, then stir in the orange juice, fruit, nuts, peel and spices.

WHISK the egg whites until stiff and fold into the margarine mixture with a metal spoon.

GENTLY fold the mixture into the noodles, spread them out in the baking dish and bake for 30 minutes until set. The top should have tempting patches of crispy brown noodles.

SERVE hot or at room temperature.

> "…a land of wheat and barley, and vines and fig trees and pomegranates; a land of olive trees and honey…" DEUTERONOMY 8:8

LEFT: OLD-FASHIONED SWEET CARROT KUGEL

Biscochos de huevo
Sephardi cookie rings

These ring-shaped cookies are served on Sabbath and festivals throughout the Sephardi world. A Turkish and Greek variation coats the cookies with sesame seeds, a symbol of fruitfulness.

MAKES ABOUT 30

3¾ cups flour
½ tbsp baking powder
½ tsp salt
3 eggs, lightly beaten
⅔ cup superfine granulated
  sugar
½ cup vegetable oil
1 tsp vanilla extract, 1 tbsp
  ground cinnamon or 1 tbsp
  orangeflower water
1–2 eggs, lightly beaten
finely chopped nuts (optional)

PREHEAT the oven to 350°F.

LINE a baking sheet (or two) with parchment paper.

SIFT the flour, baking powder and salt.

BEAT together the eggs, sugar, oil and flavoring. Gradually stir in the flour to make a soft dough. Add a little extra oil if the dough doesn't hold together enough to roll out without splitting.

TAKE a small piece of dough and lightly roll into a rope about ½ inch thick and 4 inches long on a lightly floured surface. Bring the ends together to form a ring. Repeat until all the dough is used up. (Note: It takes a little practice at first to get your hand-eye coordination working but it's not brain surgery. It's a question of feel, how big a lump to pinch off, when to stop rolling. Try a few – you'll be surprised how quickly you can become a little biscocho production line. The aim is consistency of size.)

PAINT the rings with a little beaten egg and sprinkle, if desired, with a few nuts.

PLACE the rings, about an inch apart on the baking sheets and bake for 20 minutes. Cool on a wire rack.

FOR extra-crispness (a matter of personal but impassioned preference), turn off the oven and leave for 10 minutes before transferring to a wire rack. Store in an airtight container.

Marunchinos
Sephardi almond macaroons

Soft and slightly chewy, these rich Sephardi macaroons are particularly popular at Pesach. Iraqi Jews use ground cardamom and/or rosewater instead of the almond extract.

MAKES ABOUT 24

1⅔ cups ground almonds
  (whole, freshly ground nuts
  give the best flavor)
⅔ cup superfine granulated
  sugar
1 tsp almond extract
1 egg white, whipped until
  foamy with a pinch of salt
almond slivers, to decorate
  (optional)
confectioners' sugar, for
  dusting (optional)

PREHEAT the oven to 325°F.

LINE a baking sheet with parchment paper.

PROCESS the almonds, sugar and salt in a food processor until finely ground. Add the almond extract and the egg white and pulse-process until the mixture forms a firm paste.

DAMPEN your hands and form the mixture into small balls. Space a good inch apart on the baking sheet. Press a large almond sliver onto the center of each macaroon.

BAKE until lightly colored, about 20 minutes. Cool on a wire rack and dust, if desired, with confectioners' sugar.

STORE in an airtight container.

Mandlebrot

As biscotti are to espresso, mandlebrot are to a glass of lemon tea. Both are twice-baked for crispness, but mandlebrot are richer, crunchier and generally easier on the teeth. There are numerous versions, containing chocolate, jam, poppy seeds and so on, but almonds (*mandel*) are essential. Hospitality is seen in Jewish law as a good deed, as well as a joy, and to ensure there was always something on hand to offer unexpected guests, many Jewish housewives kept a tin of mandlebrot on-hand.

MAKES ABOUT 30

2 eggs

½ cup superfine granulated
  sugar

6 tbsp vegetable oil

2–3 drops almond extract

2½ cups all-purpose flour, sifted
  with 2 tsp baking powder
  and a pinch of salt

1 cup coarsely chopped
  blanched almonds

1 egg, mixed with 1 tbsp water

1 tbsp ground cinnamon,
  mixed with ¼ cup sugar

WHISK the eggs and sugar, then add the oil and almond extract.

ADD to the flour along with the almonds and lightly mix to a dough. Refrigerate for several hours.

PREHEAT the oven to 350°F.

DIVIDE the dough in half and, with floured hands, shape each portion into long logs about 3 inches wide. Brush with the egg and water mixture, then sprinkle with the cinnamon and sugar. Place well apart on a large greased and floured baking sheet and bake for about 30 minutes until barely brown. Remove, but keep the oven on (you'll soon see why).

LET the logs cool down – until they still retain a little warmth, but not so much they crumble when cut. Then use a serrated knife to carefully cut into long, oblique slices about ½ inch thick.

RETURN to the oven (now you see why!) and bake for another 5 minutes on each side until they are just starting to crisp and turn light brown. Cool on a wire rack.

ABOVE: JEWISH BAKERY, LONDON

Zimtsterne

Cinnamon stars

Zimtsterne means "to the stars," and these delicious, chewy, star-shaped macaroons with a meringue topping are traditional among German-Jews after the Yom Kippur fast, which ends when the first stars appear in the night sky. If you can find them, use six-pointed Star of David cookie cutters.

MAKES 24–30 COOKIES

3 egg whites

pinch of salt

2¼ cups confectioners' sugar, sifted

2¾ cups ground almonds

2 tsp vanilla extract

1 tbsp ground cinnamon

½ tsp grated nutmeg

LINE a large baking sheet with lightly greased parchment paper.

WHISK the egg whites with a pinch of salt until they form stiff peaks. Gradually stir in the confectioners' sugar.

SET aside 3 tablespoonfuls of the mixture.

ADD half the almonds, the vanilla extract, cinnamon and nutmeg to the remaining egg white mixture, then gradually add enough of the leftover almonds to make the dough stick together. Gather into a ball and chill for an hour.

PREHEAT the oven to 300°F.

DUST a work surface with confectioners' sugar and roll out the paste to about ¼ inch thick. Cut out star shapes with a 2-inch cookie cutter. (You can make other shapes, but then they wouldn't be stars!)

SMOOTH some of the reserved meringue over the top of each cookie. (If the topping is not smooth enough, add a few drops of water.)

TRANSFER to the baking sheet and bake for 20–25 minutes until the tops are lightly colored, then place on a wire rack to cool. (The underside of the cookies should feel a little soft after baking.)

RIGHT: MANDLEBROT AND ZIMTSTERNE

A shop to remember

WHEN MY GRANDFATHER LEFT HOME IN ENGLAND AND SAILED FOR NEW YORK, HE COULD NEVER HAVE IMAGINED THE WAY HIS LIFE WOULD CHANGE FOR EVER. AHEAD OF HIM WAS A JOURNEY – AND A NIGHT TO REMEMBER. OR, TRY TO FORGET.

I grew up in a Jewish deli – raised in a pickle barrel, my mother would sometimes joke. My father, Maurice Hyman, would slice his mild and luscious home-smoked salmon as if he were Isaac Stern playing the violin. Children, crowding the shop on their way home from school, were always given "Jewish lollypops," small nuggets from the tail end of the salmon. Once, when my late mother was in the hospital, I knew she was on the mend when she managed to say, faintly but clearly, that maybe she could, just maybe, manage a little smoked salmon sandwich after all.

Titanic's of Waterloo Road could possibly be the world's worst business address. However, the family kosher deli business, the oldest in Manchester, England, has now passed onto the fourth generation. Nearly a century after Grandpa Joseph survived the famous disaster, the shop has become part of local history. Not that he actually chose that name for his small store; it was just that every time he walked through the immigrant Hightown district, people would stop, stare and whisper, "There goes the man from the *Titanic*." And so Mr. Titanic he remained for the rest of his life, the title handed, like a hereditary peerage, down through the generations.

I'm biased, of course, but to me the shop still has a special character. This is a business where the customers are like an extended family (of course, you do not have to like all your family), a *haimishe* bazaar where the staff shouts at customers and they shout back, where the air ricochets with jokes, gossip and Talmudic discussions on wholesale prices. Crowded, chaotic and noisy, the style has changed little since the doors first opened for business.

In 1912, Grandpa left a small dairy (i.e., a couple of cows near the railway station) and a wife and numerous children to search for better prospects in the US. He booked his passage on the "unsinkable" new ship. On the night of April 14, he stood by the rails as women and children were pushed into the lifeboats, but many passengers refused, believing the ship could never go down. Volunteers were called to man the oars, and Grandpa took his chance, passing around a hip flask of brandy that Grandma had given him before he left on the journey; several hours later they were picked up.

After arriving in the US, however, all Grandpa wanted to do was go straight home. It was six months, though, before he could face the return journey; even then his brother had to get him so drunk he passed out, waking up on-board ship after it sailed. Back in Manchester, with a little compensation money, he opened a tiny, kosher delicatessen in "a quarter of a shop." Selling milk and *kes* (cream cheese) in one corner, and pickled meat and wurst in another, the business soon grew, eventually to several shops, distributed around the family, helped by the small aura of celebrity. Anyone who survived such an ordeal, the reasoning went, must have God's blessing.

"This is not so much a shop, more a way of life. The people who come in here are like family. If you're rude, nobody takes it personally."

CLOCKWISE FROM TOP CENTER:
MAURICE HYMAN, THE AUTHOR'S
FATHER; SHOP SIGN; JEAN HYMAN,
THE AUTHOR'S MOTHER; MATZOS;
RICHARD HYMAN

My late Uncle Harry remembered how they would smoke and pickle meats in the basement: "We couldn't afford to buy metal pots in which to press the beef, so we devised the idea of rolling them in linen cloths, tying the ends with string. We would put a great weight on top; then when the meat was cold, it solidified and we would get a beautiful roll of pickled meat." My cousin Stanley's worst memories, however, are of boiling vats of calves' foot jelly, delicious but with a smell that could knock you sideways.

Cucumbers for pickling came from the Netherlands in hessian sacks. Winter was the time for salt herring, then May and June brought the fat schmaltz herring. There were always smoked fish in season, and salmon hanging in the basement like wash drying on a line.

Sunday mornings, then as now, were the busiest time of the week. The old shop would be packed and as noisy as a sawmill. Uncle Dick Raynes once told me how the lines were so long, "they'd be making up sandwiches in one corner, and selling them to customers to eat while they were waiting to be served."

Today, the old, dark houses and streets have been swept away. Scabrous housing estates, barricaded jails and pawn shops in the lee of Strangeways prison have taken their place. The present shop has moved down the road from the original site, and presents a curiously blank face to the outside world. Only the rows of cars parked three deep are a giveaway.

Despite the modern, brightly tiled interior, decorated with *Titanic* and local memorabilia, it is like entering a small, Eastern European country; the noise is constant, there are arguments in at least three languages, customers push their way through a rocky undergrowth of boxes piled high with cans of Israeli cucumbers on sale. Trays of freshly fried fish are carried out in golden relays. When hunger pains start, there is a slice of wurst or a piece of gefilte fish to munch. An elderly man in a pin-stripe suit confides to Stanley: "My doctor told me I shouldn't eat chopped liver, but you only go once, so you might as well go with the taste on your lips!" The gag is as old as the speaker.

As Stan says, "This is not so much a shop, more a way of life. The people who come in here are like family. If you're rude, nobody takes it personally. I can scream at people if they're driving me mad, and they'll just laugh and say, 'Calm down.'"

Neither Stanley nor his son Richard contemplate moving, although they have since opened two more outlets in the suburbs of north Cheshire. "Historically, there's always been a Titanic's in Waterloo Road. We're famous – twice a year the Friendship Club comes from Blackpool. They visit Heathlands (the Jewish old-age home), the cemetery, and then, as the highlight, they come to Titanic's." The success of the film has made little difference, apart from the occasional joker who asks for iceberg lettuce.

Richard, who now runs the business, has been innovative, introducing many new lines, especially ready-made meals. "Part of the reason I came into the business was to keep the tradition going. At the same time, I am trying to match the products with the professional manufacturing skills of the 21st century. We're doing a lot more, for example, with the deli counter: it takes me 13 days to make the pastrami and our chopped liver is out of this world – it sells by the bucket load!"

Stan, as ever, has to have the last word: "It's a business you've got to be born into. You've got to have schmaltz in your veins."

Jennifer Hyman's beet jam

Jennifer has made this recipe for *eingemacht* (beet jam) every Pesach since she married my cousin Stanley in 1966. She got the recipe from her grandmother, Annie Glass, who was eight years old when she came in 1900 from a town on the Polish-Austrian border. "She was very proud of the fact her jam had a golden rather than red color, due to her use of brown sugar and the fact she peeled the beets before boiling them." Jennifer still uses Annie's preserving pan and spoons: "She's with me every time I cook it – it's a better way of remembering her than visiting her grave. I do it exactly the way she did – all by hand. There may be quicker ways, but this will always be my way."

MAKES 5-6 PINTS JAM

7 lb beets, peeled

4lb 8oz granulated sugar

6 lemons

1 heaping tbsp ground ginger

large handful of whole
    blanched almonds

BOIL the raw beets for about 1 hour until you can just get a fork through them. Drain (use the liquid for borscht) and set aside to cool.

CUT into wedges then into small, even, triangular shapes. "Annie was very insistent they all had to be the same size."

PLACE in a large saucepan with the sugar and about ⅜ cup cold water. Heat gently, stirring frequently to make sure the sugar doesn't catch. Once the liquid starts to come out of the beets, turn up the heat so it bubbles gently.

PLUNGE the lemons into boiling water and drain. Peel off the skin and pith and cut into ½-inch slices, then into quarter triangles. Discard the pips (this also helps clean red-stained fingers).

AFTER the beets have been cooking for 1 hour, add the lemons. Keep the jam bubbling away, then after another 30 minutes add the ginger. Continue to cook for another 1½ hours until thick and jam-like, although remember it will thicken even more as it cools.

TO determine if the jam is ready to fill, drop a teaspoonful on a chilled plate. Let it sit briefly then push gently with a fingertip; if the surface of the jam wrinkles, it is ready. (Take the pan off the heat while you are testing.)

THROW the almonds in at the very end, and mix well. Pour into warm, sterilized jars. Cover and label when cold. Eat on matzo; "It doesn't taste right on bread."

Index

Selected bibliography

Jennifer Felicia Abadi, *A Fistful of Lentils* (2002, The Harvard Common Press)

Albert Arouh, *A Taste of Sephardic Salonika* (2003, Fytrakis)

Molly Lyons Bar-David, *The Israeli Cook Book* (1968, Crown Publishers Inc)

Chaim Bermant, *The Walled Garden* (1974, Macmillan)

Chaim Bermant, *Murmurings of a Licensed Heretic* (1990, Peter Halban)

John Cooper, *Eat and Be Satisfied* (1993, Jason Aronson Inc)

Mitchell Davis, *The Mensch Chef* (2002, Clarkson N. Potter)

Ruth Gay, *Unfinished People* (2001, Norton)

Joyce Goldstein, *Cucina Ebraica* (1998, Chronicle Books)

Joyce Goldstein, *Sephardic Flavors* (2000, Chronicle Books)

Florence Greenberg, *Florence Greenberg's Jewish Cookbook* (1980, Hamlyn)

Gloria Kaufer Greene, *The Jewish Festival Cookbook* (1988, Robert Hale)

Daisy Iny, *The Best of Baghdad Cooking* (1976, Saturday Review Press)

Vera Komissar, *Jødiske Gleder* (1988, Luther Forlag)

Robert M. Levine, *Tropical Diaspora* (1993, University Press of Florida)

Gil Marks, *The World of Jewish Cooking* (1996, Simon & Schuster)

Gil Marks, *The World of Jewish Entertaining* (1998, Simon & Schuster)

Gil Marks, *The World of Jewish Desserts* (2000, Simon & Schuster)

Joan Nathan, *The Jewish Holiday Kitchen* (1988, Schocken)

Joan Nathan, *Jewish Cooking in America* (1994, Alfred A. Knopf)

Joan Nathan, *The Jewish Holiday Baker* (1997, Schoken)

Joan Nathan, *The Foods of Israel Today* (2001, Alfred A. Knopf)

Milka Belgrado Passigli, *Le Ricette di Casa Mia* (1993, Giuntina)

Claudia Roden, *The Book of Jewish Food* (1997, Viking)

Evelyn Rose, *The Essential Jewish Festival Cookbook* (2000, Robson)

Evelyn Rose, *The New Complete International Jewish Cookbook* (2000, Robson)

Leo Rosten, *The New Joys of Yiddish* (2001, Crown)

Mira Sacerdoti, *Italian Jewish Cooking* (1993, Robert Hale)

Oded Schwartz, *In Search of Plenty* (1992, Kyle Kathie)

The Sisterhood of Mikvé Israel-Emanuel, *Recipes from the Jewish Kitchens of Curaçao* (1982, Drukkerij N.V.)

Arnold Zable, *Cafe Scheherazade* (2001, Text Publishing)

Picture credits

The publisher would like to thank the following photographers and agencies for their kind permission to reproduce the photographs in this book:

4 left Museum of the Jewish Diaspora (Beth Hatefutsoth Photo Archive); 5 left David Silverman/Travel Ink; 8 left Mike Poloway; 8 right Chris Caldicott/Axiom Photographic Agency; 10 Robin Laurance/IMPACT; 11 picture Courtesy of Tita Mendes Chumaceiro/Museum of the Jewish Diaspora (Beth Hatefutsoth Photo Archive); 13 above center Gregory Wrona/Panos Pictures; 13 above right S. Molins/Hutchison Picture Library; 13 center left Clarissa Hyman; 13 center right David Silverman/Sonia Halliday Photographs; 13 below center Yosefa Drescher Photography; 16 PA Photos; 17 left G.Wrona/Panos Pictures; 17 right Scala Scala; 22 right Ian Lillicrapp; 23 left Museum of the Jewish Diaspora (Beth Hatefutsoth Photo Archive); 25 above center Masha, John & Lisa Zeleznikow; 25 above right Masha, John & Lisa Zeleznikow; 25 center left Bill Bachman; 25 center right Robert Francis/Hutchison Picture Library; 25 below center Bill Bachman; 26 Masha, John & Lisa Zeleznikow; 34 left N.Haslam/Hutchison Picture Library; 34 right Jonathan Smith/Sylvia Cordaiy; 37 Clarissa Hyman; 38 Lesley McIntyre/Hutchison Picture Library; 55 Christophe Bluntzer/Impact; 57 above left Clarissa Hyman; 57 above center and center left World Pictures; 57 center right World Pictures; 57 below center Clarissa Hyman; 58 Abraham and David Recanati Collection, Tel Aviv/Museum of the Jewish Diaspora (Beth Hatefutsoth Photo Archive); 59 Lucy Mason/Anthony Blake Library; 64 and 65 above left Michael J. O'Brien/Panos Pictures; 65 above right Michael J.O'Brien/Panos Pictures; 73–74 Clarissa Hyman; 77 E.Simanor/Axiom Photographic Agency; 85 Clarissa Hyman; 86 Jeremy Horner/Hutchison Picture Library; 92 Christine Osborne Pictures; 94 David Silverman/The Travel Library; 97 above center Jane Taylor/Sonia Halliday Photographs; 97 above right Billie Rafaeli/ Hutchison Picture Library; 97 center left David Silverman/Sonia Halliday Photographs; 97 Yosefa Drescher Photography; 103 above left Janet Wishnetsky/Impact; 103 above right Robert Francis/Hutchison Picture Library; 104 above left Barry Searle/Sonia Halliday Photographs; 119 above center Stuart Black/The Travel Library; 119 above right Clarissa Hyman; 119 center left Clarissa Hyman; 119 center right Stuart Black/The Travel Library; 119 below center and 120 Clarissa Hyman; 125 Jeremy Horner/Hutchison Picture Library; 126 Sonia Halliday Photographs; 128 Jane Taylor/Sonia Halliday Photographs; 129 J.C.Tordai/ Hutchison Picture Library; 133 above center Steve J.Benbow/Axiom Photographic Agency; 133 above right Florian Profitlich/AKG London; 133 center left Paul Quayle/Axiom Photographic Agency (Designed by Daniel Libeskind); 133 center right Clarissa Hyman; 133 below center Dieter E.Hoppe/AKG London; 134 Clarissa Hyman; 136 left Benjamin Hertzberg, USA/Museum of the Jewish Diaspora (Beth Hatefutsoth Photo Archive); 136 right Clarissa Hyman; 142 Mike Poloway; 149 Ian Lillicrapp, England/Museum of the Jewish Diaspora (Beth Hatefutsoth Photo Archive); 153, 154 and 160 Clarissa Hyman.

Every effort has been made to trace the copyright holders and we apologize in advance for any unintentional omission and would be pleased to insert the appropriate acknowledgement in any subsequent edition.

LEFT: ESTHER AND JOSEPH
HYMAN, THE AUTHOR'S
GRANDPARENTS

Acknowledgements

I would like to thank all the Jewish "network," my friends and family
who generously gave me time, help and recipes.
Special thanks, however, must go to:
Leon & Albert Arouh, Gita Conn, Ruth & Charles Gomes-Casseres,
Ruth & Yitz Greenwald, Cass Chaya Hirsh, Jennifer Hyman,
Aron Kelton, Vera Komissar & Julius Paltiel, Alan Marcuson,
Norma Raynes, Rabbi Walter Rothschild, Laila Rubens,
Rabbi Ruben Silverman, Lisa Zeleznikow and Shiri Ziv.

In great appreciation of their assistance in making my journeys
around the Jewish world possible, I would like to thank:
KLM, the Avila Beach Hotel and Curaçao Tourism Development
Bureau; Lufthansa, The Aston Hotel, Berlin-Mitte & Michael Helmerich
of the German Tourist Office; VLM, The Hotel Prinse, Antwerp & Dawn
Page of Tourism Flanders-Brussels; Olympic Airlines; SAS.

Many thanks also to Michele Barlow, Christine King, Lorna Rhodes
and KitchenAid for invaluable help with the recipes; to Peter Cassidy,
Jacque Malouf and Megan Smith for making my vision of
The Jewish Kitchen a beautiful reality; and to Katey Day for constant,
sympathetic support and encouragement.